MARKETING

UNWRAPPED

RAY PERRY

JOHN WILEY & SONS, LTD

New York · Weinheim · Brisbane · Singapore · Toronto

Other Wiley Editorial Offices

John Wiley & Sons, Inc., 605 Third Avenue,
New York, NY 10158-0012, USA

Wiley-VCH Verlag GmbH, Pappelallee 3,
D-69469 Weinheim, Germany

John Wiley & Sons Australia Ltd, 33 Park Road, Milton,
Queensland 4064, Australia

John Wiley & Sons (Asia) Pte Ltd, 2 Clementi Loop #02-01,
Jin Xing Distripark, Singapore 129809

John Wiley & Sons (Canada) Ltd, 22 Worcester Road,
Rexdale, Ontario M9W 1L1, Canada

British Library Cataloguing in Publication Data
A catalogue record for this book is available from the British Library

ISBN 0-471-48694-9

Typeset in 12/16pt Bembo by Footnote Graphics, Warminster, Wiltshire
Printed and bound in Great Britain by Biddles Ltd, Guildford and King's Lynn.
This book is printed on acid-free paper responsibly manufactured from sustainable forestry, in which at least two trees
are planted for each one used for paper production.

CONTENTS

Acknowledgements
I should like to thank Claire Forbes, Dawn Southgate and Catherine Haveron
for their help and support in creating this book.

Dedication
To Jaymin and Sabrina

FOREWORD

Many management disciplines and skills are currently having to change and adapt to the new environment of business in the twenty-first century. Marketing is no exception; it has to change, and indeed is changing. Shareholders, stakeholders and owners of businesses increasingly require added value from the organisation. The starting point has been creating economies of scale and scope, with processes becoming more efficient and resources utilised more effectively. But whilst all these process activities are undoubtedly important, it is highly likely that your competitors are doing exactly the same thing.

In the end what will make the difference between you and your competitors is creating and driving brands successfully, through innovation and knowledge management. This should be the new heartland for the marketer. Whilst still managing the day-to-day activity of marketing management, marketers need to learn new skills. They need to build knowledge and focus; they need to manage relationships with the customers and indeed the supply chain. To achieve this, marketers will have to become more measurable, so that the company can value the contribution. In return, companies will need to become increasingly focused on the customer and the process more marketing-driven. If the marketing is right, the desired financial results will follow.

This book sets out to specify the new challenges and roles that the marketer should be aspiring to create and develop, with practical and helpful guidelines. By developing the professionalism of marketing, and championing customer focus at all levels of the business, the end game is much more likely to be achieved, namely more predictable success, greater understanding of brands and the market, and added value driven by the marketing team. It's a tough challenge but perhaps, after reading this book, it's a challenge that many more marketers will take on board.

Sir George Bull
Chairman, J Sainsbury plc

INTRODUCTION

Open any business magazine, or flick through any business book published in the last twelve months and at some stage you're almost guaranteed to come across phrases like: "fast pace of change" or read how things are "moving faster than ever before". It may not be original to say it – but it's true.

Most professionals expect to manage their place in this changing world by learning new techniques, abiding by the new rules, and sharpening their skills from time to time. Continuing Professional Development (CPD) is the latest three-letter acronym sweeping across the business departments, and all it really means is keeping your professional skills and knowledge up-to-date.

As a relatively new profession, I contend that the marketing fraternity has had to evolve the necessary skill sets over very little time, as well as continually changing and adjusting to market evolvements and customer needs. Unlike, say accountants, lawyers or architects, for instance, the ever-shifting sand under the marketer has meant that just as soon as the knowledge base, core skills needs, and job roles have stabilised, whoosh, here we go again – a whole new need set – category management skills, customer relationship management, affinity marketing, customer service guarantee levels.

When I joined Dunlop in 1982, I felt that the cacophony and diversity of backgrounds from which people bounced into the marketing profession was amazing. This was commonplace in most FTSE 100 companies and was synonymous of the profession. Most marketers at that time seemed to be either ex-salesmen who didn't make the next grade, or accountants, planners, print buyers or researchers who were all having a dabble in marketing. A professionally trained marketer was a rarity, as indeed was professional training. The relationship between the advertising agency and blue chip companies seemed paramount as it involved a leap into creativity, escaping the tactical drudge of the day-to-day stuff and, cynically, provided a pleasant and generally liquid lunch.

The embryonic love children of such relationships were the suit (account manager) and luvvies (the creatives). The bigger the budget, the more abstract the creative (and often more irrelevant to the product being advertised). Products that won advertising awards often didn't sell and no measurement, benchmarks, or metrics existed to confirm whether or not companies were cost-effective, or really driving either brand image or sales. Accountants took umbrage at the perceived unaccountability and waste of resource (i.e. money) in the marketing department.

This scenario was echoed in 1999 with the many "e" start-ups which spent large amounts of shareholders' money, targeting TV audiences and other media with the precision of a blunderbuss. Sadly, agencies in pursuit of a fast buck were all too happy to allow this to happen, hence the definition of an "e" start up as "the process by which venture capital funding is converted into advertising agency profits."

Partly as a result of the 1970s and 1980s learning curve, marketing received a bad press. Marketers became ponytailed luvvies, "marketing tactics and ploys" became something used by disreputable con-artists. Even today, marketing and PR "spin" is a negative label, widely seen as being the process by which government press officers bewilder, beguile and mislead both journalists and the public. "Focus group" has a similarly negative connection, as daytime TV relishes the exposure of the "professional" focus group participants (rather like the "professional" daytime TV studio guest).

Marketing is a much maligned activity. Even the Blair government – the government of the focus group and spin-doctors – failed to refer to the word "marketing" once in its 1998 White Paper on Competitiveness.

So the profession has had to find its feet on the shifting sands, joggling tactical and strategic priorities, cutting through the minefield of bad press, and in many cases, let's be honest, bad marketing.

How do we stop mistakes from, say, the 1960s happening again? There would seem to be minimal knowledge shared in most companies. Take the comment by Chris Hawken, marketing director of Skoda – named Marketer of the Year in 2000.

> In the past there has been no consistency in [Skoda's] advertising and it is our fault. We haven't used any of our data. There's loads of it out there – fleet, customer and prospect – and it's all just sitting there, getting dirty (from Campaign 16.07.99).

Very few marketers, if any, chart the hits and misses down the years. There are two reasons for this:

1. If it doesn't work, push it under the carpet.
2. If it doesn't work, leave.

Research suggests that the average stay at any company for a product manager is between 18 months and two years. What can anyone do in that time except make one major mistake, or have one success?

What the profession has lacked is what it takes to make a profession. A codified knowledge base, definition of skills and tasks required, strategic as well as tactical focus, training and personal development, and finally measurement.

Towards the end of the last century, many companies began the professionalisation of marketing; companies such as Kellogg, Unilever and Procter & Gamble began internal training and development schools. Strategy units began talking in marketing speak, buzzwords abounded in the 1980s and 1990s. The classification of "what marketing is" began with the likes of Kotler's "Marketing Management", Ansoff's Diversification matrix, and Porter's five forces and supply chain models. These economists who specialise in demand-side economics morphed into marketing professors, and structure and focus began to grip the profession through training and business schools.

Professional institutes including the big two – The American Marketing Association (AMA) and The Chartered Institute of Marketing (CIM) in the UK and Asia – developed accredited learning, diplomas and training schools. Business schools began to focus on marketing, including the Massachusetts Institute of Technology (MIT), Northwestern University and Harvard Business School in the US and Cranfield University, Warwick University, Henley, Stirling University and London Business School in the UK. Simultaneously, companies such as General Electric and IBM, under Lou Gershner, began programmes of company-specific training for marketers so that global standards could be set for different levels of management.

The basic marketing toolkit evolved, broadly speaking, into that shown in Figure I.1.

Strategic marketing	P.E.S.T.L.E.	Consider Political, Economic, Social, Technological, Legal and Environmental issues
Process	MOST	Define Mission, Objectives, Strategy and Tactics. Linked through supply chain
Competitive environment	5 forces (Porter)	Plot the power of suppliers/buyers/ new entrants/substitutes/ key players
Marketing audit	SWOT	Identify Strengths, Weaknesses, Opportunities, Threats
Marketing plan	SMART objectives BCG Model 4 P's (or 7 P's)	Seeing products as either stars, dogs, cash cows or problem children. Resultant strategy plan for Product, Price, Promotion, Place (plus, for service brands, Physical evidence, People, Process)
Action plan	Brand communications mix	Deliverables against timeline
Internal marketing	Stakeholder map	Split stakeholders into high/low by power versus interest

Figure I.1 Dynamics of the marketing role.

Now, at the beginning of the twenty-first century, several statements can be made.

1. Marketers have stopped being the dumping ground for burned-out salesmen.
2. The profession has become more codified.
3. The core skills, at least in large companies, involve a mix of tactical and strategic abilities.

4. Training and development of marketers has become generally acceptable and inevitable.
5. Marketers, whilst their activities are still not measurable the way an accountant's are, have gained some respect internally.
6. Marketers are still seen as inwardly focused, insular and not driving the bigger picture. They are too tactical rather than strategic.

So, one might think as a profession that we have won game, set and match – true? No, sadly those shifting sands are back on the scene. Just when marketers thought it was safe to look down, it's all change again.

In the twenty-first century, issues that face marketers as they struggle to shape up to challenges include:

• Pan company marketing – for many of the roles we shall discuss it is increasingly necessary for marketers at all levels to engage all internal shareholders, to "buy-in" to activity, and recognise there is a marketing element in all departments' roles,
• Measurement metrics – how marketers should track and measure performance,
• E-commerce – understanding the language of the IT team to develop Websites and e-CRM,
• Knowledge management – what to, and how, to store information, who has access?
• Integrated Supply Chain Management – the Web marketer,
• Customer Relationship Management/Interface,
• Multi-channel activity in the connected economy message and media selection.

The reality is that marketing is becoming more holistic. Everyone in the company has to think of themselves as a marketer and consider who their customer is and what they are delivering to them. This results in two essential ingredients in the marketing skill set which were not apparent in the twentieth century:

1. *Interpersonal skills – working with different departments and stakeholders.*
2. *Project management skills – keeping a firm grip on what is happening across brands and divisions.*

A good way to look at the marketing department of the future is to consider multi-tasked, project focused, functional teams of managers with specific product/service profit responsibility, but also a matrix of specialist skills which will involve relationship building with stakeholders from other departments and even other organisations.

Based on this matrix structure, this book will explore elements of the skill sets and core competencies necessary to develop and train employees, in search of the holy grail of marketers:

Where maximum profit = maximum consumer satisfaction

An example of a matrix structure is shown in Figure I.2, whereby marketers take on a pan departmental role as well as their current brand role. Here different skills are learned, so that by the time aspiring marketers reach board level they are assumed to have developed these skills on their route to the top. Obviously, the smaller the company the fewer the staff, and therefore, marketers would have to take on more matrix roles as well as their brand responsibility. In a very small enterprise, outsourced agencies or consultants would be enlisted.

Fictitious Plc – with seven brands and matrix skill structure

Matrix skills

	Relationship marketer	Media marketer	Supply chain marketer	Knowledge marketer	Partnership marketer	Metrics marketer
(Board Director Marketing Manager)	X	X	X	X	X	X
(Category/ Brand Manager 1	X					
(Category/ Brand Manager 2		X				
(Category/ Brand Manager 3			X			
(Category/ Brand Manager 4				X		
(Category/ Brand Manager 5					X	
(Category/ Brand Manager 6						X

Figure I.2   An example of a matrix structure.

These roles could be seen as a process, as in Figure I.3 below.

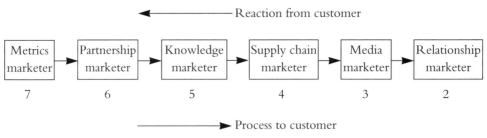

Figure I.3   Customer-focused roles in the connected economy.

This book will not focus primarily on the existing functional skills required for marketers. These are taken as implicit in the brand manager role, for instance, new product development (NPD), market research or marketing planning. If this is an area of interest, Appendix 1 discusses the Skills Level Analysis Process (SLAP) which is a joint venture between Marconi and the Chartered Institute of Marketing (CIM), describing the level of skills and understanding necessary for traditional job roles. In addition, Stopgap and CIM have published a marketing job description guide called "The Marketing Workplace". This is free to members at www.cim.co.uk, or available to purchase.

I will focus on the future, and look at what every marketer needs to know in order to succeed. As well as the traditional functional role, marketers will need to be flexible, adaptable and multi-skilled, ultimately gaining all the skills identified in the matrix structure above.

Chapter 1 will outline the transition into the new economy and its impact on the marketer. Subsequent chapters will pick out a specific matrix skill and explore the dynamic environment in which the role will operate, the reasons for this new requirement, and the benefits.

Each chapter will conclude with the following:

• The Role – Reason for the role and its scope and objectives.
• The Strategic Fit – Who the key stakeholders are in relation to this role and who the customers are.
• Core Competencies – the core competencies required to succeed in this role, and critical success factors.
• Summary and further reading.

USEFUL SOURCES

Davidson, H. (1997) *Even More Offensive Marketing*, Penguin.

Dibb, S., Simkin, L., Pride, W. and Fennell, O. (2001) *Marketing Concepts and Strategies* (4th European edition), Houghton, Mifflin.

Doyle, P. (1998) *Marketing Management and Strategy*, Prentice Hall.

Harding, S. and Long, T. (1998) *MBA Management Models*, MPG, Cornwell.

Kelly, K. (1998) *New Rules for the New Economy*, Fourth Estate, Harper Collins.

Kotler, P. (2000) *Marketing Management*, international edition, Prentice Hall.

HELPFUL WEBSITES

www.AMA.org – This is the American Marketing Association, and has useful content with a US perspective.

www.cim.co.uk – This is a UK portal for marketing, with content, provided by the Chartered Institute of Marketing.

www.connectedinmarketing.com – This site is focused on issues relating to e-marketing.

THE TWENTIETH-CENTURY PERSPECTIVE OF MARKETING SKILLS AND COMPETENCIES

THE TWENTIETH-CENTURY PERSPECTIVE OF MARKETING SKILLS AND COMPETENCIES

There has long been a conflict over the marketing role since it means all things to all people. The easiest way to begin is with the standard definition from The Chartered Institute of Marketing (CIM):

> Marketing is the management process responsible for identifying, anticipating and satisfying customer requirements profitably (Peter Blood, CIM Annual Report, 1976).

What the role actually includes, however, can vary tremendously across the dynamics shown in Figure 1.1, and depends on the type of company and its environment.

Clearly, the operating environment influences the dynamics of the

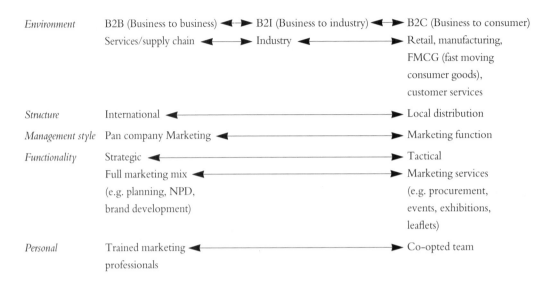

Figure 1.1 The marketing role in various types of company.

marketing role, and therefore the required skill base. But equally the management philosophy and style has a major input. There is an argument that the whole company has both internal and external customers, not just the marketing department. Add to that a company-wide mission and suddenly everyone from the cleaner to the chief executive is involved in marketing.

In practice, of course, the mental picture of an accountant wishing to live the brand values of the organisation and delight their marketing budget holder with exemplary service may seem far-fetched. Similarly, the IT department's speed to service might not fit the wants and needs of a front-line operator in customer services. One of the greatest inhibitors in a call centre, for instance, is screen downtime.

Functionally, a global manufacturer such as toy company Mattel Inc would view each country as a distribution point at which tactical marketing would be required. For a local service provider, for example British Midland, customer service is much more important and the marketing less tangible, but more strategic.

So when we talk about marketing roles, there is a need to be very specific.

CLASSICAL MARKETING

In 1974, Peter Doyle of Warwick Business School stated:

> To many people, marketing represents the least respectable side of business. At the same time, it is the area which demands perhaps the maximum flexibility and individual commitment.

There was a good deal of confusion about the role of marketer and salesman, and indeed, where one started and the other finished.

This was Lord Stokes' view in 1969, as Chairman of British Leyland:

> Marketing should be your strategic planning linked with the logistics of supply. Selling should be the tactical exercise, coupled with your front-line troops, the infantry as it were, of the industrial world, without whom nothing effective can be accomplished . . . No matter whether it be motor cars, machine tools or baby foods, the methods of production and the equipment used in modern factories in most countries of the world today are remarkably similar. So this really leaves us with two variables – [labour relations] and secondly, the question of marketing which to my mind embraces planning the product strategy for the future.

What a shame that British Leyland failed to overcome the first hurdle, and never managed to link marketing to the customer need, or supply chain. British

Leyland were, as history suggests, sales- rather than marketing- or customer-driven. This was synonymous across most industries which experienced blurred boundaries between sales and marketing: a sales focus masquerading as customer focus. This is still true of many companies today.

Marketing departments tended to be marginalised rather than margin focused. Professor Michael Thomas stated:

> Marketing as a discipline is more vital than ever, marketing as a department is increasingly failing to match up to expectations. The marketing department is critically ill; only urgent treatment will enable it to fulfil the role that is now clearly staked out in the minds of top management.

- Marketing departments undertake an ill-defined mixture of activities,
- Marketing departments have been over-indulged,
- Marketing departments rarely lead the drive to enhance business performance,
- Marketing departments are often too short-sighted,
- Marketing departments are being marginalised,
- Marketing directors and managing directors disagree,
- Marketing directors overestimate their contribution.

Even in the 1970s a familiar cry echoed across the business community:

Q. What do marketers need to do to become more professional?

A. They need to come to terms with finance, and they need to demonstrate that they are the professional experts in respect of marketing information and as a consequence we must come to terms with Information Technology.

It all sounds very familiar. Pre-1950s the relationship with the consumer was generally on a local level, with little functional marketing. However the marketing function drove the rise to power of consumer goods companies. Everybody else was swept along as manufacturer's brand fought manufacturer's brand for dominance. During this period marketing drew its power from two principal sources: innovation and a company's relationship with customers and consumers. In parallel the spread of television and the introduction of commercial channels allowed manufacturers to develop a new kind of relationship with consumers.

The marketers, especially in FMCG markets, began to see the retailer as the customer at the expense of the end consumer and user. This reached a peak in the early 1990s, and is described in the seminal article, "Marketing's Mid-Life Crisis", by John Brady and Ian Davis:

> In the old days, marketing concentrated on the consumer; today its attention is on the trade. Consumer goods companies spend large chunks of their marketing budgets on providing trade promotions and doing trade deals. Overlooked in this process, the consumer is often short-changed. Tomorrow's marketers will be known for their focus on both parties, as they identify and support the linkages between consumers and retail outlets, and attend to the whole shopping experience. Equally important will be their ability to interpret consumer and retailer needs, and to keep tabs on how – and how far – their products meet those needs.

Marketers with the ability to plan end cap/gondola end displays with the retailer, manage advertising agencies, and balance a research portfolio on sales and usage were deemed "classically trained marketers". Customer service was not the priority of marketers; the movement of product was paramount. Job descriptions reflected the segmentation of task, not customer, clusters. The training was generally on-the-job, in the field, enacting time-honoured practices in sectors such as FMCG, Durables, or Motor Manufacturing.

Ironically, there were often very few marketers at all in retail or service companies, who were actually at the customer face.

WHAT ABOUT THE NEW RECRUIT?

The titles of marketing jobs have barely changed over the last 30 years. All the roles have had one thing in common – they are all company-focused and inward-looking, and not customer-focused. Figure 1.2 gives some examples.

Typical titles	Task
Product manager	Profit, quantity shipped
Category manager	Profit per square foot/metre
	Customer, not consumer focus
Key account manager	Trade focus
Customer service manager	Managing retail complaints

Figure 1.2　Company-focused marketing titles.

What sort of people were being recruited for the task in the 1970s and 1980s? Let's take a look at real job adverts for marketers twenty or thirty years ago:

- Product Manager
  Ideally a graduate in your mid to late 20s with some three years experience in a blue chip FMCG company, you will be joining a marketing team of young, aggressive professionals used to standing on their own performance.
  Marketing Week, 1979

- Marketing Manager
  A married person in their early thirties is preferred ... *Marketing Week*, November 1979

- Marketing Manager
  Autonomous company, £8 million turnover in ladies fashion, part of a major group, is looking for a sales orientated businessman/woman with formal marketing training. The post would suit a graduate who has done his stint with the big boys and now wants to work at top level without frustrations next to the managing director. Someone with the right common sense and enthusiasm could be next in the chair. – *Marketing*, June 1980.

Seemingly, business wanted blue chip experience, sales orientation and maturity in a marketing manager skill set. Generally, there was little focus on the functional requirements of the profession. But in academia, a tradition of classical training had begun in the 1970s when marketers were encouraged by CIM, AMA, universities and others to study marketing planning rather than economics.

In the 1960s the CIM diploma required aspiring marketers to study economics, geography and business history. It wasn't until 1975 that the diploma included, for the first time, the now familiar subjects of Marketing Planning and Control, Management Organisation and Communications, and Marketing Analysis and Decision.

What was not being taught was leadership skills. To be a real success in marketing you will need to have, or develop, those human qualities which are generally thought of as being the most essential ingredients of the leader – arguably, intelligence, integrity, moral courage, enthusiasm and the human touch.

This shortage of suitably qualified professionals was not limited to the marketing profession. Professor Ray Wild of Henley Management College noted in 1974:

> Industry and commerce have persistently asked for more realistic business school graduates. They claim to seek individuals who not only understand the complexities of the environment in which an organisation operates, its corporate policy etc, but who are able and anxious to do a job of work below board level. It might on occasions appear that graduate knowledge has become an end in itself – an unproductive, introverted relationship, at least as far as industry and commerce is concerned.

THE CURRENT MARKETING ENVIRONMENT

There are a number of factors which are influencing the way marketers are currently operating, and these have implications for the future.

The Future Environment

In the 1970s we were operating in a commercial environment in which packaged goods reigned supreme. Privatisation was unheard of, advertising spend in the UK was £800m compared with £8bn today, there was one commercial TV channel, no media independents, and national newspapers used nineteenth-century print technology.

In the following two decades, we have seen customers being persuaded to use brands in more varied and different ways – eating breakfast cereal at night, taking out supermarket-branded credit cards or mortgages, drinking branded vodka and cola whilst flying on an aeroplane with the same brand name.

Things have changed dramatically – twenty years ago almost every business document was produced on a typewriter. Communication across the world was difficult, time-consuming and unreliable. Far fewer people took foreign holidays or had cars; supermarkets were open from 9am–5pm; and cash machines were almost unheard of.

At the end of the 1980s, the CBI produced a report entitled: "Towards the twenty-first century – prospects for the UK in the 1990s". It identified the key trends likely to occur amongst consumers in the 1990s, some of which are highlighted below:

1. People expect to get richer and to consume more material goods; but they are also likely to want to look beyond materialism with an increasing interest in quality of life.
2. Economic factors are likely to lead to the emergence of more "super-rich", a larger "middle class" and possibly an increasingly impoverished underclass.
3. Some will move beyond materialism through participation in various forms of non-established religions, meditation and relaxation, while others will seek refuge in drugs.
4. Demographics are likely to lead to more old people and fewer people seeking their first job.
5. Political decisions will increasingly be made in Brussels and in other international groupings rather than Whitehall.
6. Political power in the UK will be dominated by whoever can best persuade the electorate that it can marry continued economic prosperity with an improved quality of life.

At the same time, the now defunct *Sunday Correspondent* newspaper did something similar, but they approached consumers themselves, asking them which items they expected to have in their household in ten years' time. While 5% were convinced that they would have a fully functioning robot in their homes today, some of the other answers were more revealing. Fifty-two per cent of people expected to have satellite TV in their homes. The actual figure in 1999 was 17.5%. Fifty-one per cent expected to have a computer in their homes – the actual figure was 23%.

The same survey asked people how many hours they thought they would be working per week in ten years' time, and the answers showed an expectation amongst consumers that they would have more leisure time, not less. Table 1.1 shows consumers' expectations of leisure time.

And yet, as we all know, we are now working more hours than ever before, and the British work the longest hours in Europe. What is interesting is that neither survey predicted the enormous impact that the Internet has had on our society, or the huge proliferation of media and communications channels that are now available at the touch of a button.

Today's consumers and marketers also face a new dilemma: confusion. Confusion in the marketplace, confusion in the media, confusion in the shops, confusion about where to shop and even how to shop. It's a confusion that results from an excess of choice. The Henley Centre describe it well: they say that the world has become "blurred".

Table 1.1   Hours workers thought they would be working in ten years time compared to today (% of sample).

%	Men	Women
Fewer	70	66
Same	24	26
More	6	9

Immediacy

Ira Matathia and Marian Salzman in "Whatever Next?" a predictive article published at the end of the twentieth century, noted that the last hundred years had seen the global adoption of automobiles and electric lights, men walking on the moon and advances in medicine that extended average life expectancies into the 70s or 80s. They wondered what might the next century bring. As they suggest, immediacy is a major issue – anything that's not immediate is s-l-o-w. We want same-day delivery, instant news, microwave meals, direct TV and PC banking.

Changing Demographics and the Grey Market

A recent BMRB–TGI survey states that there are now 5.3 million more adults in the UK than there were thirty years ago. At that time, one-third were in professional occupations; today, two-thirds are in professional occupations. Similarly, thirty years ago, 12% went to university while today, 25% go to university.

Two-thirds of the population have no children living at home. Twenty-two per cent of housing stock is used by single adults, due to the rise of divorce and single parenting. There have been major increases in home ownership. Part-time working is more prevalent, especially amongst women, and 76% of adults have access to a car. Over one-third of adults have two or more cars.

It used to be that people over 50 were old, and people under 30 were young. Throughout much of Europe and North America, women are now delaying childbirth until their thirties or forties. The arrival of Leo Blair in 2000, to a forty-something mother, set the seal of respectability on older motherhood.

Adults are running around in tennis shoes and shorts, working out at the gym in an attempt to delay some of the normal ravages of ageing – and having plastic surgery to mask much of the rest. The fashion industry has been forced to redesign its "youth" fashions to fit the bodies of the middle-aged men and women who continue to wear them, rather than adopting more "grown-up" fashions. Take Marks & Spencers recent attempt to revitalise its image – "I'm size 16 and I'm normal!", or Levi's recent adverts featuring a 75-year-old woman wearing jeans. Men and women in their 70s and 80s are remaining physically (even sexually) active, travelling the world, and are sometimes involved in running companies – and countries.

In the years ahead, it is inevitable that the world's "elders" will command unprecedented attention from marketers and the media, and will have an enormous impact on the rest of the population. The reality is that we're entering into an era in which the elderly will make up a larger proportion of the global population than ever before. Already, the most rapidly growing age group is made up of those aged 85-plus. In the US, this group will double in size by 2025 and increase fivefold by 2050. Around the world, half of all people aged 65 and over who have ever lived are alive today.

Our ageing population promises to influence everything, from financial planning and home design to the way products are made and sold. As the number of elderly continues to increase, so will this group's power in terms of influencing public policy. Images of the elderly as victims will become historical; instead, we will see seniors who grow more active in politics and who maintain and even increase their economic power as they move into their second half-century of life. Socially, politically – and certainly economically – the implications of this development will be felt by us all.

The impact on marketers is that they need to thoroughly research markets, segment into niche markets, avoid broad blunderbuss campaigns that are bland, generic, and aimed at the average person.

Borders? What Borders?

Borders are a twentieth-century invention. Bronze Age men traded copper and bronze artifacts in borderless Europe. For cross-border travellers in Europe, things are just returning to where they were a century ago, when it was possible to wander across the Continent without a passport.

Worldwide, geographical borders disappear in cyberspace and, consequently, marketers have to design and market products across borders and consider the impact of, for instance, differential pricing in different territories. A policy of selling the same goods at half-price in Asia, for instance, may come back and haunt you, as many luxury goods manufacturers have discovered, when supermarkets such as Asda began to import their products into the UK at a lower price.

The impact on marketers is that they need to think more globally, keep international knowledge management systems, and involve all territory marketers in strategy development.

Privacy, Data Protection and Spamming

Loss of privacy is a common fear today. Governments are concerned at the invasion of individual privacy by fax, phone, mail, and e-mail spamming. Legislation has now come into force to protect the consumer, allowing him to receive copies of all the information a company holds on him.

When your bank or credit card company potentially holds details of everything about you from your political affiliations to your sexuality, the 'big brother' scenario of Orwell's *1984* becomes alarmingly close. Not only will consumers become more wary about what personal information they give out (and what they allow companies do with it) but personal information about consumers will have a price, with consumers demanding discounts and reductions on products and services in return for divulging more details about their lives and preferences.

The impact on marketers is that they need to build brands sympathetically to customers and set best practice in permission marketing, by only giving the potential customer information if they request it and by acting as the customer's guardian when releasing (or selling) data.

Alternative Ways of Working

Although many companies would deny a trend towards virtuality, the reality is that they're already heading in that direction. There is likely to be a dramatic increase in the amount of business communication conducted virtually, whether by intranet Web-conferencing or via videophone. Telecommuting, sometimes called teleworking or homeworking, is already common in the US. In Europe, there currently are 1.25 million telecommuters, a number that is expected to increase dramatically as the telecommunications infrastructure is improved. Workers will begin to rely less on corporate loyalty and more on their own skills – and the opportunities new technologies afford – and more and more of them are setting up shop on their own. Eurostat reports that approximately half of small to mid-size businesses in Europe are one-person companies.

The impact on marketers is that more marketers will work from home, sub-contracting matrix skills will become more common. There is a strong need to build good remote communication and team-working skills.

Humans Replaced by Computers

Analysts predict that by the end of the twenty-first century, employment as we know it is likely to be phased out in most of the industrialised nations of the world. For the first time in history, human labour is being systematically eliminated from the economic process. A new generation of sophisticated information and communication technologies, together with new forms of business reorganisation and management, is wiping out full-time employment for millions of blue- and white-collar workers.

Just as manufacturing jobs were taken over by robots in the 1970s and accounting/finance jobs were taken over by batch-processing computers in the 1980s, middle-management jobs have been under siege in the 1990s. A key reason is advances in technology that have moved information out of the exclusive possession of management and into the general population.

The impact on Marketers is a need to show their value to the organisation with metrics and campaign measurement, systemic benchmarking against competitors.

Proliferation of Media

Changes in attitude towards media are now more prevalent. Consumers will switch service providers on the Internet, surf a plethora of digital TV channels, search the Web. The pace of media change is moving increasingly quickly.

The recent increase in media channels has provided advertisers with an increase in commercial viewing. According to John Billett speaking at the Marketing Forum in 1999, commercial TV viewing has doubled in the last thirty years (as has commercial radio). As the population becomes more mobile, more opportunities in outdoor advertising have developed. Cinema has recovered spectacularly while there has been a major decline in daily newspaper exposure – there are now 12 million fewer readers than there were twenty years ago. Only 60% of people read a paper today. Magazine readership is also down – 30% compared to twenty years ago. There has also been a decline in football pools and bingo.

There has also been a major shift in attitude towards the media as the list below shows:

Enjoyment of TV ads – declined
Expectation of TV to keep people informed
Relaxation in front of TV – in decline
Increased cash spent on TV – average annual spend on media is £239 per person
TV takes over half adult media spend
Internet spend is still relatively small

A number of critical factors emerge from this:

- Fragmentation of audiences – more media
- Explosion in number and type of opportunities of new media
- Mergers amongst media owners are prevalent
- Consolidation of agency groups/media buyers
- Increasingly hard to analyse media success across the large variety of media
- Direct response and electronic measurement are increasing

The impact on marketers is that they need to understand the dynamics of all available media and generate communication strategies that, cost-effectively, hit the segmented target. No one agency is currently capable of achieving this.

The dot.com Impact in Today's External Environment

The dot.com environment changes every day and by the time this book is published any information or statistics I attempt to quote will be out of date. What won't change is the impact that the Internet is having on the way in which business operates. As Laura Mazur, one of the UK's most respected marketing journalists, said in 1998: "Build on an idea as quickly as possible, growth is more important than profitability, speed is more important than stability. Go for it or get left behind."

The traditional business ethos has been turned upside down by the advent of the Internet, and many of the subsequent chapters in this book will be exploring the dot.com phenomenon in greater detail. However, a business can't survive in the dot.com era without:

1. A realistic, profitable, SMART business plan.
2. A customer-focused marketing strategy.

Whilst many dot.com companies have failed, many could have survived with greater marketing expertise and brand building.

From a marketing skills perspective, marketers need to see the Internet as a strategic business transformation and a new channel to market, both of which allow marketers to build new business and better one-to-one relationships with new and existing customers.

WHICH SKILLS DO MARKETERS NEED TODAY?

Earlier we looked at job advertisements from twenty years ago. We will now consider those from 2001:

- Head of Direct Marketing
  ....You must be skilled in strategic planning, using databases, negotiating contracts and working at a senior level. You should also have a record of providing creative solutions to a variety of marketing problems and working with IT specialists to achieve the most appropriate support for marketing needs.
  The Guardian, Media Supplement, December 2000.

- Web Communications Manager
  We're looking for someone with creative spark, vision, drive and exceptional editorial and online design skills. On top of that, you'll need a really strong grasp of corporate identity as well as first-class management experience and networking skills.
  The Guardian, Media Supplement, December 2000.

A SWOT OF MARKETERS

Before looking closely at skills analyses, if we look back at marketers over the last 30 years we could carry out a SWOT analysis on the profession. (SWOT stands for Strengths, Weaknesses, Opportunities and Threats.) Below are my suggested results for a typical marketer.

Strengths:
Bright
Ambitious
Challenge the status quo
Creative

Weaknesses:

Do not engage the entire business

Weak measurement tools

Weak people skills

Short tenure in one company

Opportunities:

Exploit strengths – be bold, creative, strategic and innovative

Champion the cause of the customer

Sell themselves

Talk to other functions

Develop new measurement tools

Threats:

Failure to compete with potential

Finance/operations domination

Failure to harness IT

Failure to harness customer service

Ignore the trends. Does not change

LACK OF SKILLS, COMPETENCIES AND TRAINING

The Synesis Report of 1997 was a study billed as an audit of the marketing profession. It aimed to find out how the profession thought it was doing, where it is heading and how well equipped marketers believed they were for the future. It revealed that marketing was a self-confident profession with high self-esteem. This is striking, since it conflicts with concerns expressed by marketing directors in previous marketing forum research. In these studies marketers have said that they are worried about the future of the profession and want to re-examine where it is going. They lacked IT skills and competencies, and had failed to grasp the concept of customer service.

Marketers often don't act as a team with the rest of the business. Further, a number of factors seem to be endemic to marketing teams in all sectors:

a) Lacking breadth
Marketing people prefer to advance their own professional development rather than broaden their career within the company. It is most common to recruit from outside the company (40–60% of positions are filled this way).

b) Engagement
HR teams criticised marketing teams for failing to engage the business in what they do.

c) People Skills
Marketers also have strong internal competition. Operations, sales and finance compete well for the attention of the business – their careers are built on people skills, they are skilled in internal politics, and use measurements and IT facilities to demonstrate the effectiveness of what they do.

A critical implication is that the organisation needs to identify the skills it requires from marketing people and ensure that staff have the opportunity to develop them. A recent CIM survey revealed that only 41% of marketers are satisfied with the recognition they receive. HR directors feel that marketing teams could assert their role in a more effective manner and be clearer about what they are trying to achieve.

According to Synesis, marketing managers are seen to be stronger at creative and analytical stuff than at people and influencing skills. Only 26% of HR directors felt that marketing teams engage the rest of the business in their plans, and many felt that they could do this better.

Seventy-eight per cent of marketers rated themselves as good or excellent at working cross-functionally, whereas only 23% of their colleagues thought the same. Primary complaints were that marketing teams were not good enough at analysis or measurement (18%) and did not communicate with the rest of the business when developing or launching their plans (23%).

When asked "Which skills do you have formal training in?", marketers answered as follows (see Figure 1.3):

Sales promotion – 16%
New media – 19%
Creative advertising – 21%
Media strategy and buying – 25%
Brand strategy – 35%
Market research – 38%
Direct marketing – 41%

Marketers would like to develop specific areas, particularly those in the new areas of new media and brand strategy, while preferring to learn the core activities of advertising, direct marketing and promotion through on-the-job training.

Marketing teams must develop new skills and operate in different ways if they are to deliver this role in an effective manner. We still have some way to go to convince the business we are as effective as we might be. It is essential that marketing teams earn the respect of business so that the whole business becomes market-led.

The key to this would seem to lie in new communication skills and having

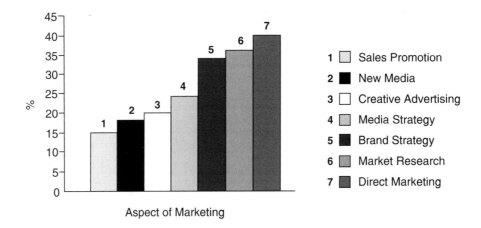

Figure 1.3 The percentage of marketing people with formal training in specific areas.

robust tools for identifying opportunities, analysis and measurement. Without this, creative brilliance and smart analysis will lose its impact.

Another report conducted by Elliott Maltz University of Southern California looked at the relationship between the frequency and quality of contacts made by marketers with their non-marketing colleagues, the impact on the credibility of the marketing function and the subsequent market orientation of the business. This study strongly suggests that marketers who interact with their non-marketing colleagues less than ten times a week tend to have their work undervalued by other departments.

Marketing is a revenue generator for companies. Recent research from CIM showed that whereas nine out of ten British firms have a finance director on their board, only half have a marketing director. If we accept the role of marketing as a wealth creator then the lack of board presence for marketers is scandalous.

Perception of Marketers by Finance Directors

It would be relevant at this point to look at the way finance directors (FDs) view marketers. The 1998 Finance Directors' Forum assessed the relationship between finance and marketing.

Although most finance directors still believe the marketing department considers them "enemy number one", they were keen to stress that this does not colour their perceptions of marketers. Top of the list for sources of conflict were a lack of fiscal discipline, poor administration and over-confidence and enthusiasm. Their pet hates included "numbers always being rounded up to £1000", "always spending up to or over the budget", and "a lack of regular visibility in the office".

Many marketers are thought to suffer from a desire to shine at all costs, even if their pet projects are not performing well, thus reflecting a perceived lack of willingness to be held accountable for their mistakes. Common adjectives used to describe marketing people were "brash", "salesmen" − in the pejorative sense − "loose cannons", "uncontrollable" and "wide boys". Most finance directors believe marketers have an equally jaundiced view of them. They feel they are perceived to be "boring", "mean", "cautious", "risk averse", "unimaginative", and "interested in the cost of everything and the value of nothing".

On the positive side, many finance directors recognise that such criticisms are often justified. They accept that finance is partly to blame for not seeking to redress the situation. Encouragingly, it was universally agreed, particularly by younger finance directors, that the marketing department provides the lifeblood of a company and that its creative spirit is essential for business growth. They perceive that one of the key challenges is learning how to "manage" marketing. Opinion on how to do this falls into two camps: the old school and the new.

Rather than confront the conflict, the "old school" works around it. The traditional approach is to assume that marketing's forecasts were wildly optimistic and hence protect the overall budget by making allowances elsewhere. Such finance directors expect to cut the advertising budget before the end of the year to make up the difference – which is an easy way to generate instant funds without incurring a penalty. They prepare external audiences for the results they expect rather than those that the marketing department has predicted. The "old" solution is based on avoidance, resulting in a widely acknowledged compromise for both departments.

However, a new forward-thinking group of financial directors is emerging which sees an opportunity for marketing and finance to work together. Key to its thinking is communication. Almost all finance directors acknowledge that they rarely meet marketing people – often only twice a year. Regular dialogue in weekly or monthly management meetings would avoid confrontation at more formal board meetings, representing the first step towards a better relationship.

Measuring the effectiveness of advertising is considered to be a critical target. Many finance directors are educating themselves about research and measurement techniques. Today, there is much more optimism about being able to collaborate with marketing.

Interestingly, a new problem may be looming. As finance directors have successfully transferred their responsibility for information technology to IT directors, they have given them more time to take a more consultative role. They paint a picture of a future where they will "shape and measure the business", "provide a steadying hand on the tiller", and "manage shareholder value". They expect to become business facilitators and innovators.

Marketers, meanwhile, cite their three main roles for the future as "shaping the business and the market", "influencing the customer" and "operating at the cutting edge". Perhaps the true challenge for the future, as *Marketing Week* (30 July 1998) suggested, once a dialogue is established, will be fighting for the position of number two advisor to the chief executive officer.

FUTURE DIRECTIONS

The EIU (Economics Intelligent Unit) report (2000) predicted how top business organisations would look by the year 2010. Based on the views of 350 CEOs from across the globe,

- CEOs identified that new global competition and the accelerating rate of change would demand that organisations be much more flexible than in the past and do things better than ever before. A key focus for management teams will be understanding and developing their core competencies – i.e. doing the things at which they can excel, and doing them brilliantly.
- The CEOs stated that, in this situation, the forces which drive competitive advantage will not be the traditional levers of product and service quality and reducing costs, but the ability to be excellent at something (core competencies), to manage relationships and to be flexible.
- Skill sets demanded for successful executives include communication, decision making and managing relationships. CEOs seem to be much less impressed with technical skills.
- Judging by the findings of this survey, marketers are primarily focused on developing their technical expertise and have much to learn in the people arena. If we accept the views of these CEOs this seems like the wrong thing to be doing. It is likely to lessen marketing's influence and effectiveness over the next ten years.

As we have seen in this chapter, the marketer is not operating in a vacuum. All of society is changing in today's information age, and marketers need to adapt to these pressures. The key to success in e-commerce will be competitive advantage generated by using electronic means as a platform to leverage knowledge and awareness, online. Added value, especially in the business-to-business (B2B) environment is being gained through extranets, a low-cost solution for linking databases, and through collaborative networks. Information services can be clustered and shared between partners, and products bundled and linked for the retail or business customer.

LAWS OF THE E-REVOLUTION

Moore's Law states that computing power doubles and the cost halves every 18 months. Gilder's Law notes that total bandwidth triples every 12 months. It is also estimated that the utility of a network is exponential to the number of nodes in the network or, in plain English, the bigger the network the better; the more customers you get the more they add value to each other. Amazon.com is perhaps a classic example of this.

Table 1.2 below shows one view of the changes that have taken place in marketing strategy.

Table 1.2 Changes that have taken place in marketing strategy.

Twentieth century	Twenty-first century
Process management	Network
Internal focus	Customer focus
Structured or clustered	Adaptable
Fixed policies/strategy	Infinitely flexible
Buildings, investments	Knowledge/intellectual property

In addition, operations are also changing significantly, as Table 1.3 below shows.

In the twentieth century, the world was focused on producing atoms, that is, tangible solid products, while in the twenty-first century the focus is on bits and bytes. In other words, value is in information and knowledge, not in production. This will have a profound effect on marketers. There will be core changes in how we view strategy, as shown in Table 1.4.

Alan Mitchell in *Marketing Business* (February 1993) said: "To say the marketing department is responsible for marketing is like saying love is the responsibility of one family member." This was echoed by Terry Leahy, Chief Executive of Tesco, Britain's number one retailer, who stated: "Marketing is something I try to do every day. It's something that the business tries to do every

Table 1.3   Changes in operations between the twentieth and twenty-first centuries.

Operations	Twentieth century	Twenty-first century
Products	Mass production	Mass customisation
Markets	Domestic	Domestic and global
Market statistics	Monthly/ad hoc	Real time, point of interaction
Inventory	Months	Just in time (JIT)/Made to Order
Strategy	Top-down	Middle-out/customer-in
Leadership	Control paradigm	Customer led
Workers	Employees	Stakeholders
Job expectations	Cradle to grave	Training/flexible Individual, focused
Motivation	To compete	To build
Improvements	Incremental	Swift step change
Quality	Industry standard level	Meet customer expectation

Table 1.4 Changes in strategy from the twentieth to the twenty-first century.

Twentieth century	Twenty-first century
E-commerce gold rush	Community development
Spend, spend, spend	Cost efficiency, metrics, benchmarking
Get there first, go it alone	Pick right partners, sustainable model
Loyalty and CRM focus	Revenue models, permission marketing
Functional approach	Matrix approach, multi-tasking, multi-skilling. Pan company marketing
Product approach	Service focus
Segment markets	Segment customer clusters

day. It's not about a function or the department – it's the whole organisation and everybody who's in it."

In subsequent chapters we will use the matrix from the introduction to look at the way marketers' core skills will need to develop to reflect the needs of today and tomorrow, to produce customer focus, profitability, and added value across the organisation.

SUMMARY

1. Environments have changed due to technology.

2. Customer expectations now lead marketing

3. Marketers have to become more interactive with other stakeholders and drive customer-added value.

4. Marketers have to become more measurable, and adopt a pan company approach, through matrix structures.

5. Marketers need a longer term perspective, and need to build brands.

USEFUL SOURCES

BMRB-TGI survey, www.brmb.co.uk

Brady, J. and Davis, I. (1993) Marketing's Mid-Life Crisis, *McKinsey Quarterly* **12**, 17–28.

Doyle, P. (1974) *Education for Marketing*, Marketing Forum.

Elliott Maltz University Report (see Maruca, R.F. (1998) Getting marketing's voice heard, *Harvard Business Review*, Jan–Feb, 10–11.

Economic Intelligence Unit, Vision 2010 Report, "Designing Tomorrow's Organisation".

Guardian Media Supplement, Head of Direct Marketing job advertisement, 11 December 2000.

Matathia, I. and Salzman, M. (1999) "Whatever Next", *The Guardian*, 9 January, p. 30.

Marketing Week, November 1979, Classified Jobs.

Marketing Week, June 1980, Classified Jobs.

Marketing Week, 30 July 1998, "Rivals for the Purse Strings".

Mitchell, A. (1993) Marketing Business.

Synesis Report (2000) "You Can't Get the Staff these Days".

Williams, D. (1990) "Towards the 21st Century – prospects for the UK in the 1990s", Confederation of British Industry.

TRAINING

www.cim.co.uk – All marketing.

www.idm.co.uk – Direct marketing. This is the site of the Institute of Direct Marketing in the UK.

www.ipa.co.uk – Advertising.

www.mrs.org.uk – Market research.

HELPFUL WEBSITES

www.mckinseyquarterly.com – The site of the journal of global consultants McKinsey.

www.mad.co.uk – The site of Centaur Publications, who produce marketing-related magazines.

www.synesis.co.uk – A site that produces research and feedback on marketing issues.

THE CUSTOMER
RELATIONSHIP
MARKETER

THE CUSTOMER RELATIONSHIP MARKETER

T his chapter considers the new significant importance of the role of the Customer Relationship Marketer. We will look first at the way markets are changing, and why the focus of leading companies is on the consumer. We will ask what Customer Relationship Management (CRM) and electronic CRM (e-CRM) are and examine their value, and indeed, whether they work. We will consider whether or not they are for everyone. We will then look at the implementation of CRM, what can go wrong, and the extent to which CRM techniques have been adopted. We will reflect on the best ways to manager a customer relationship and establish the golden rules of CRM. Finally, CRM is compared to electronic CRM, leading to an analysis of the role, fit, and competencies that are necessary to succeed in this role.

Once upon a time it was possible to create a great brand, with a good product offering, and as long as no nasty competition came along, you could promote your product to stimulate sales, but you did not have to worry much about the customer.

American circus entrepreneur P.T. Barnum relied on the premise that "there's a sucker born every minute". Once his show was over, he did not expect his customer to come back, and a new sucker had to be recruited. However, in today's business environment, retaining customers is crucial to a company's success.

Even as recently as the 1990s the customer did not used to be viewed as a stockholder, he was not considered to be involved in the process, and therefore, there was no need for a Relationship Marketer function. Companies invested to some extent in database management systems, but any interaction with the consumer was a by-product of collecting the figures.

These days the success of a company depends on its successful strategic interaction between internal stakeholders, in pursuit of external recipients: yes, the customer. Whereas once it was relatively easy to innovate and create unique selling professions (USPs) around your product or service, two things have changed.

1. *The post-Internet customer has more choice than ever before.*
2. *Cost reduction is finite, so being cheapest is not sustainable for long.*

The choice available to consumers or customers is vast and many boundaries have blurred. Companies with a recognisable brand have built trust amongst their own customers so well that when they cross a boundary the customer still buys from them. Examples include the Virgin ISA, vodka or trains, Sainsbury's Bank or easyJet car hire. So the importance of bond building cannot be under-estimated as a lever to consumer trust, confidence and acceptance of brand promises where your product or service is neither the cheapest nor established within the niche.

DEFINITION OF CUSTOMER RELATIONSHIP MANAGEMENT (CRM)

First, we need to define CRM:

> Customer Relationship Management (CRM) is developing into a major element of corporate strategy for many organisations. Also known by other terms such as relationship marketing and customer management, CRM is concerned with the creation, development and enhancement of individualised relationships with carefully targeted customers and customer groups, the desired result being to maximise the total customer lifetime value. Professor Adrian Payne, from Customer Relationship Management, CBI (November 2000).

Another view is expressed by Ron Swift as follows:

> Customer Relationship Management (CRM) is an enterprise approach to understanding and influencing customer behaviour through meaningful communications in order to improve customer acquisition, customer retention, customer loyalty and customer profitability. Ron Swift.

With these in mind, we will now look at customer loyalty programmes.

CUSTOMER LOYALTY AND AFFINITY MARKETING

Myth "All I need to do to build a relationship with my customer is introduce an affinity card – giving points for prizes, discounts, etc".

Wrong! This is a short-term promotion which buys the short-term attention of buyers. All things being equal, they will continue to purchase your goods. Are customers loyal to the points on their loyalty card, or to the service?

American Express customers may use the card to accumulate points, but their experience of the service the company provides may still tempt them to defect. Promotions are, therefore, just part of the marketing mix. Loyalty is not just an action: it's a state of mind. Customer loyalty is about trust and such programmes can only ever be a support act.

The real issue is to decide whose loyalty is worth having: it is necessary to match the customer's current profitability with potential future profitability and intention to re-purchase. Generating true loyalty is a long-term process and loyalty is often a response to "soft issues" such as brand commitment and emotional attachment, rather than hard facts. In the US for instance, communications company AT&T found customers felt that emotive issues associated with the brand were more important than service satisfaction. Loyalty is habit – you can't buy loyalty – but you can create a habit.

A good example of building a habit is the Boots loyalty card.

Example: **Boots Loyalty Card**

- Take-up of the card exceeded expectations and generated profits after nine months.
  Eight million cardholders were engaged, but at a cost – £5–6 million in extra costs.
  The customer data has been used to target Boots Mother and Baby at Home catalogue.

- Boots say that the card has produced an estimated £60 million of sales as a result (source: *The Times*, 5th June 1998). In total, 39% of all sales were linked to the card.

So clearly cards can work, but companies should make sure that:

1. They are viewed as a promotion, and not "real" loyalty.

2. The costs of attraction and running are calculated and deducted from additional profit.
3. They are aware that sales will fall when the promotion stops.

The best form of loyalty doesn't flow from a smart card, but comes from trust in the brand – brand loyalty.

BRAND LOYALTY

One of the long-term sustainable benefits of building a relationship with the customer is to build brand loyalty. The term "loyalty" is often taken out of context. It is not at one end of the scale, a cradle-to-grave bonding, or at the other end a supermarket affinity programme. There is little loyalty in either scenario. Loyalty in a brand context means that, given a consistent market niche, for instance flights to New York, and given two comparable products, the established customer would require a very good reason to switch brands from his regular first choice. However, if there is a good reason, he would switch in an instant, provided there is minimal hassle in doing so. It is the latter that has stopped many people from swapping banks despite appalling customer service and unreasonable bank charges. The same has traditionally been true of other state monopolies in utilities and telecoms. It is the relationship marketers who must build the relationship and trust in the brand through a continuing programme of Customer Relationship Management (CRM).

WHAT IS CUSTOMER RELATIONSHIP MANAGEMENT?

Before defining the relationship marketer's role, we need to understand CRM.

Myth "CRM is just about buying a piece of computer software which will manage my website (e-CRM), and help me run offline promotions (CRM).

Wrong – Technology doesn't buy loyalty. It does, however, get you to the starting grid.

According to AMR Research (source: *Marketing*, 11 November 1999) sales of CRM systems reached £1.6 billion in 1998 and that figure is projected to rise to £10.5 billion by 2003. This technology helps to handle mass communications and process customers:

1. *CRM packages* will help to identify clusters of customers with similar profiles, buying patterns and behaviour, alluring you to analyse and target each segmented niche with appropriate messages to help maximise sales per customer.
2. *e-CRM packages* help to target individuals online, in order to offer them targeted promotions, based on their use of the Website and practising patterns.

But it's not just a matter of plugging in a package and doubling revenue. Research by the Gartner Group (source: *Marketing* 11 November 1999) concluded that in some CRM sectors, up to 65% of projects failed to deliver and many overran or came in over budget.

However, to be successful a brand needs to deliver:

• quality and Reliability
• value for money/marketing pricing

- excellent service and customer contact
- excellent back-up
- online delivery
- service and guarantee
- salience – the right product to satisfy market need.

All these depend on good marketing and people. Technology is just a lever, a mechanism, a fixed cost of business, like a shop to a traditional retailer.

Customer Relationship Management is the process of getting to know who customers are, understanding their behaviour and needs and then driving profitability through more efficient marketing communications and high customer retention. It is growing in importance because of the rise in consumer power (ignore your customer's needs at your peril – we all know the Marks & Spencer story).

It is the coming of age of direct marketing – companies have learned how to collect data, and now that data is being used to optimise customer relationships and improve profibitability.

> *Example*: The Woolwich bank recently scrapped its product-based marketing teams and replaced them with a centralised structure to target groups of customers with multiple products. Head of Group Marketing Paul Birkett said: "A marketing strategy based on CRM means that none of our firepower will be wasted by offering inappropriate services".

From a marketing and strategic perspective, customer loyalty, CRM and one-to-one marketing – whatever you want to call it – depends on finding out everything possible about your customers, and then building an appropriate and profitable relationship with them.

At the moment, CRM is being delivered as a method of combining one or more of the IT systems that exist or can be placed into an organisation. This normally includes the following:

- data warehouses
- customer service systems
- call centres
- e-commerce
- Web marketing
- operational systems
- sales systems.

The idea is to integrate all these systems together so that the organisation can manage its customers. There is no doubt that CRM can be a major factor in achieving competitive advantage. It could be argued that there are three prongs to a CRM approach: strategy, marketing, and IT.

Does it Work?

Well, let's look at the evidence – as we intimated earlier, customers do not owe loyalty to you. Frederick Reichheld discovered that 15–40% of customers who say they are satisfied with a company defect each year. Ninety-eight per cent of unhappy customers never complain, they just switch to another supplier. Similarly, it has been estimated that it costs five to seven times more to find a new customer than it does to keep a current one.

It is also noteworthy that "totally satisfied" customers are six times more likely to re-purchase over one or two years than "satisfied" customers. K.R. Bhote noted that a 5% reduction in customer defection can result in profit rises of between 30 and 85%. Increasing customer retention by 2% is the equivalent to cutting operating expenses by 10% (K.R. Bhote, *Beyond Customer Satisfaction to Customer Loyalty*).

A research programme by Bain and Co. concluded that a 5% increase in customer retention can result in a doubling of profits. Research by the Direct Mail Information Service shows that mailing to existing customers achieved response rates 50% higher than mailing to people who had made enquiries to the company in the post and then lost contact (that is, lukewarm contacts). Finally, when mailing to rented lists (cold contacts) the return was only one-third of the return gained from existing customers. Nine per cent achieved more than a 30% response rate, and 4% more than a 50% response. Thirty-seven per cent of companies with a customer database say they have achieved higher levels of customer service (Softworld Sales and Marketing Annual Survey 1999).

So the short answer is, yes, it does work. A specific focus on the customer will yield the benefit of extra profit. The trick is, however, to spend a disproportionate amount of time and effort on your best customers. Consultants McKinsey concluded that not all customers are important. They suggested that some 30%–40% of an average company's revenue is generated from customers who are unprofitable if judged on a stand-alone basis, while a study of retail banking concluded that 50% of customers generate no profit at all. Companies should respond appropriately to all levels. A good CRM system will, for example, link the most profitable customers with the best sales and service support.

IS CRM FOR EVERYONE?

CRM is more widely used in consumer than business-to-business campaigns. Research from the Direct Mail Information Service shows that 79% of consumer campaigns target people on an existing database, compared with 67% of business-to-business drives. Twenty per cent of consumer marketers will use rented lists, compared with 23% of business to business marketers. In both cases, the majority of marketers use existing customer lists as their primary source. In some sectors, customer marketing dominates direct mail, and all campaigns by credit card companies, banks and building societies and luxury goods companies only mail to names on their customer database. Finally, in the leisure and entertainment sector, 89% of companies used customer databases, compared with 88% in travel and 86% mail-order companies.

The midmarket demand for CRM solutions is booming. According to Meta group, between 30 and 40% of growth in the market will be driven by companies with between 50 and 1000 users. If big companies consistently deliver good service, customers will get used to it, and so small companies as well as large ones have to take action to retain customers.

IMPLEMENTATION

There are a number of emerging issues around the implementation of CRM:

1. The implementation of a successful CRM programme is a long-term investment, involving new IT systems, changing business processes and retraining of staff. Peter Simpson of First Direct said: "The whole CRM thing is becoming a bit of a fad rather than a well thought-out strategy. It's not a bolt on strategy. Companies need to take a holistic approach."

   Example: At British Airways, all customer information is now stored in the same place and updated continually so that customers never need be asked for the same information twice. Emma Chablo of Smartfocus said: "CRM takes years to implement in a big company like BA. The cultural change is almost as big a job as the technology itself."

2. There is often a conflict between the short-term goal of balancing budgets and the long-term objectives of the business. However, marketers can prove that good returns are possible from better campaign performance.

   Example: Thames Water wanted to sell water softeners which would cost £900, a price which not everyone would be able to afford. By using a sophisticated CRM system to target prospects, they were able to increase response rates 12-fold.

3. Whilst various functions in a company such as sales, marketing, IT, finance and research will have their own views on what is best for the business, it is important that the project does not become bogged down. It must have a well-defined scope and strategy that focuses on the core benefits of CRM. Cultural resistance must also be overcome, and departments must be encouraged to share information.

   Example: Kardex encouraged use by piping sales leads through the CRM system rather than distributing them via hard copy – those who did not log on missed out.

4. For CRM to work, a company must unleash people's commitment by giving them the freedom to try out their own ideas and make a difference to results. Many managers are uncomfortable about releasing control in this way.

5. The company needs to make sure that it has a process of continuous data-gathering at customer touch points (the Net, phone, direct mail, etc). That data has to be turned into knowledge to understand customers and predict their needs. This information should be available to all staff in customer-facing operations.

6. Data must be valued as a key business resource by all staff at all levels, e.g. a call handler needs to be able to recognise an implementer, a decision-maker, a regular contact or an occasional purchaser. John Cooper, a Royal Mail consultant, said: "If the caller is treated like a new customer every time, then your business is really missing a trick."

7. Indiscriminate data-gathering clogs the system. Data collected must be vital data.

8. Surveying customers' opinions is not enough. Good CRM tracks actions as well as words.

9. Andrew Greenyer of The Database Group says that successful CRM depends on the three C's:

   - correctness – is data used validated and clean?
   - clarity – the system must be easy to use, such as a windows-based system.
   - cost – the project must be manageable and geared to the size of the business.

10. Keep all options open – while companies need to allow customers to contact them by whatever method they prefer, research by Brann Contact shows that 86% of people still prefer to telephone a company rather than contact it via the Web.

11. When Web technology is used, it must be part of a well planned strategy. Mark Huey of the Meta Group said: "The key thing is to do everything you need to do to turn the Web into a channel." Huey cites the difference between insurance companies who ask Website visitors for details and then call them back, and those that have reinvented the process by, for instance, allowing customers to compare quotes in real time.

GETTING IT RIGHT – AND WRONG

Sadly, the marketing community has not risen to the challenge of controlling the customer interface. John Merry of Coca-Cola says that lack of confidence among marketing managers has enabled a number of unscrupulous suppliers and consultants to rebrand old products as CRM and offer a "one product fits all" solution. But the solution must fit the company's needs. Richard Clarke, a financial marketing consultant, believes that companies need to ask, "What is it that our customers want?" and not "How can we improve our service to our customers?". Indeed, a customer relationship leader will not be satisfied with doing things a certain way because "they have always been done that way". Processes must be challenged.

The danger that we have identified is that CRM is often viewed as a software package, and not a business process that demands investment. Many initiatives do not use applications that promote real collaboration with customers. David Owen, CRM practice leader at Deloitte Consulting, states that consumers will expect a shift towards new technology in the next few years. However, "it is not just the technology, but what you do with it that enables you to survive and thrive in this new 'clicks and mortar' economy". In the future, the market for CRM technology will be dominated by three or four major suppliers, like other software markets. CRM buyers must future-proof their systems and ensure that they do not choose a doomed vendor.

There are two key risks emerging from this:

• According to research from Mitchell Madison Group, financial situations are wasting billions of pounds on CRM by focusing on the wrong areas. The study suggests that top-heavy allocation on non-core customers is the root of the problem.

- CRM also carries a risk. What if the customer does not want a relationship? Marketers must ensure that all interaction is welcome interaction by a thorough understanding of the customer.

Nevertheless, CRM is important. Marketers have to embrace technology both on- and offline to gain strategic advantage by knowing the customer better.

Industry Attitudes

In an interview of 131 business managers for the Business Intelligence report "Measuring and Valuing Relationships", 53% were found not to know what the term CRM means.

However, in a recent survey, 77% of executives said CRM was becoming a top priority in their business (Thyfault, 1998), while a survey of IT managers found that improved customer service was the number one business priority for the use of technology.

A survey of visitors to the Direct Marketing Fair held in London in March 2000 showed that 95% said they needed CRM software to support their marketing database.

The Softworld Sales and Marketing Annual Survey (1999) questioned 120 members of the CIM. Fifty-five per cent of companies said they were planning to review their sales and marketing IT systems within the next 12 months. A large percentage was unhappy with their existing systems, and one in four was not satisfied with the performance of their IT. Less than half had customer databases, but 63% were planning one within the next three years.

However, according to a survey carried out by MBO Solutions, there is a gap between the hype and the reality of CRM. Eighty per cent of marketing and services directors have done nothing to implement policies.

But is the industry keeping pace with consumer expectations and the development of the Internet? David Owen of Deloitte Consulting said:

> [Our research] shows the technology gap between consumers' awareness and their adoption of new technology and new channels is shrinking and that, as a result of this, European consumers are now signalling a wake-up call to business. There is clear evidence of a pent-up "permission pool" – where for the first time consumers are showing signs of a massive willingness to be communicated with and sold to across these new channels. Forty-three per cent of European consumers already say that remote technology fits with their lifestyle.

MANAGING CUSTOMER PROFITABILITY

Clearly CRM efforts must integrate analysis across all functions and channels to pinpoint those customers and tap their full potential. However, the investment case for CRM applications remains soft because:

- many operational packages offer limited analytical strength
- serious quantitative analysis remains a speciality market
- internal data provides only a partial, static, customer view.

Firms must manage customer profitability. It is often agreed that ultimately there are no unprofitable customers, only poorly managed companies. Firms must model customer behaviour, turn analysis into action and revise constantly to maximise each customer's profit. To support their needs, today's static, data-oriented CRM systems must add action-oriented analytics to calculate the investment needed to retain the best customers.

THE GOLDEN RULES OF CRM

1. Companies must create a customer-centric organisational structure.
2. Don't expose field employees to raw profitability information; marketers must package it.
3. Uncoached line employees with access to raw profitability data may adopt a new – and potentially demeaning – attitude toward less rewarding customers. Rein in these tendencies by communicating policies detailing how profitability data should be used.
4. Share profitability gains with customers.
5. Augment the marketing team with manufacturing service and distribution experts.
6. Activity-based costing gives way to customer-based costing in tandem with the accounts department on customer management.
7. Provide marketers with customer-level profit information.
8. Privacy obsession will hurt European profitability metrics; be prepared.
9. Low-profitability customers will revolt – unsuccessfully.
10. Ensure all databases are co-ordinated and synchronised – in real time.

Example: The American Automobile Association recently provided a "chilling" example of the impact unsynchronised information has on the treatment of profitable customers. One AAA member called them when he ran out of gas one cold night in northern Vermont. "This was my first call to AAA in six years of membership. I was put on hold while they verified my status by calling the three different states I lived in, which have different computer systems. After three frigid hours, I spent $100 on a towing company instead. I'm done with the AAA." The result: the firm lost a lifetime customer after his very first transaction with the company.

USING THE WORD "CUSTOMER" VERSUS BEING CUSTOMER-FOCUSED

It's not that long ago that train companies in the UK were greeted with a mixture of scepticism and derision when they started referring to passengers as "customers". A reflection, perhaps, on the notoriously bad service offered by the UK train companies?

But now, everything is customer-focused. Suddenly, telephone lines become "customer carelines", we have the introduction of "customer charters", "customer relationship management" and "customer research". As consumers we're at the heart of every business strategy – nothing, it would seem, is too much trouble. Customer care is one of the buzzwords of the late 1990s.

Mystery shopping has become a widely used technique, as have surveys of call centres, e-mail response times and shop staff attitudes by journalists and the media. There is nothing more the consumer likes than to read about the failures of big companies to do something as simple as answer a telephone with a human voice, or reply to a letter within seven days.

Example: A well known UK women's magazine recently conducted a spoof test on customer carelines: they rang four or five customer carelines, presenting a series of bizarre scenarios to each, and reported verbatim in the magazine on how each conversation went. They rang a pet food manufacturer with an enquiry as to whether or not this particular household name brand of cat food was suitable for human consumption. The operative in the call centre gave the standard answer about cleanliness on the production line and high quality ingredients. . . together with the disclaimer: "But we don't recommend it for human consumption."

"Well," said the caller, "I'm just a bit concerned, as my granny has an open tin of your cat food in her fridge – and she doesn't have a cat."

Full marks go to this particular operator, who rang the caller back shortly afterwards with the number of her granny's local Meals on Wheels service.

And then there was the customer care operative for one of the leading brands of soap powder who answered a call from a person asking how to wash blood out of a shirt. But when the operator enquired how big and old the bloodstain was, she was informed that the bloodstain was still fresh, as the body was still bleeding.

"Yes," says the caller, "he's lying on the kitchen floor with the knife still in him. Should I attempt to remove the knife before mopping up the blood?"

You have to have sympathy as well as admiration for the operative, whose next question was: "Can you give me your name and address for our files?"

WHAT DOES CUSTOMER CARE ACHIEVE?

The most loyal customers are those who have been unhappy and complained – and had their complaint dealt with to their satisfaction – they have received customer care beyond the routine standard processes that any company can offer.

Customer care helps companies to build relationships with customers. Customer service is commonly perceived as being about solving problems, apologising where necessary and responding quickly to the customer's needs – but to be really outstanding a more proactive approach is required, along with a move towards building relationships with customers.

Customer care has become a major means of differentiation between companies, especially in sectors where products are fundamentally the same. Airlines and supermarkets, for example, focus their advertising and brand management around delivering superior customer service.

THE CONCEPT OF THE "CUSTOMER"

The concept of the "customer" has permeated every aspect of twenty-first century life. At a macro level, the UK government has become more concerned about its "customers" too, setting up focus groups, carrying out research and passing an increasing amount of legislation aimed at making customers more informed and companies more accountable.

At the company level, we have the internal customer, our employees, and as managers we need to market to them as carefully as we market to our external customers. The bottom line is, to the outside world the staff are the brand.

There's been an explosion in customer-focused television programmes – surely the ultimate recourse of any disgruntled UK customer is to write to BBC's *Watchdog* programme, and succeed in naming and shaming their least favourite company during Britain's prime-time viewing. And, of course, most recently, we have had the advent of the World Wide Web, and the implications for remote customer service: without any voice or face-to-face interaction at all.

Customer care these days is demanded and expected. The consumer wants it instantly, via the method they choose and at the time they want. At the same time, customer care has become more automated, and, when not performed properly, more annoying and frustrating.

Example: Take the example of a telecoms company, you know the one, ringing a customer at the weekend or in the evening, offering special call tariffs, discounts on calling certain numbers, and so on. The telephone company knows which numbers the customer calls most – it's all there in their records. They know, better than the consumer, which tariffs would suit you best. But in the name of customer service and customer relationships they call you. This is customer dis-service.

WHAT DO CUSTOMERS WANT? HOW DO THEY MAKE PURCHASING DECISIONS?

Fifty per cent of consumers don't make price a priority for where and when they shop. According to the UK Henley Centre, British consumers are the least price-sensitive in Europe. Price is only one component of the value-for-money calculation shoppers make. People make decisions about where and how to purchase, not just for money and customer service, but also on "value for time".

Research done in 1998 by the UK Marketing Forum asked customers "What are you looking for from companies"? The research came up with clear and perhaps predictable answers. People wanted companies to:

1. Be honest and fair in dealings with them.
2. Be honest and truthful in advertising.
3. Provide good and consistent service.
4. Treat all customers fairly.
5. Treat all employees fairly.
6. Be open in providing details about the company.

The whole concept of trust came out overwhelmingly as the one thing that customers want from companies they deal with. Any concept of a relationship with a customer must be built on trust. The Marketing Forum asked how much people trusted 25 named companies on 12 different aspects, from environmental issues to honesty and truthfulness in advertising. The results of their survey are below.

Sixty-one per cent trusted companies to be honest and fair in their dealings with them (top performers: M&S, John Lewis and Boots), while 66% trusted companies to provide a good and consistent service (same top performers) and 54% trusted companies to be good at handling complaints about product and services (same performers). Fifty-six per cent trusted companies to treat all customers fairly (same performers).

Over a third of companies – 39% – are not trusted by consumers to be fair and honest. Of the 25 research participants, 41% of their budget was spent on customer acquisition, while only 23% of the budget was spent on customer retention.

So we are moving to a world where experience is as important as the product. In fact, large organisations lose 10–15% of their customers each year. A poorly handled service failure usually cuts repurchase intentions by half. What's more, 60–80% of customers who defect are actually satisfied with their previous supplier.

To provide good customer service – to keep the customer satisfied – we need to understand customer preferences for interactions and experiences. This helps identify unspoken needs and create different, sometimes unexpected beneficial experiences. Some customers prefer to manage their own relationships with us – don't call me, I'll call you. They're likely to be cynical of our attempt to build relationships with them. And if they perceive our relationship-building to be false, they'll reject them, and us, and the products and organisations we market.

CALL CENTRES ARE FAILING CUSTOMERS

Research shows very mixed results in levels of customer service satisfaction. Generally, call centres are failing their customers. For example, when telephoning a company you already do business with, you want the person on the end of the telephone to have all your details – but according to Forrester Research, only 1 in 50 companies can do this. The other 49 put you on hold, ask you the same question again, or despatch you to another operator.

Table 2.1 shows the results of a recent survey of major UK call centres.

Table 2.1 The results of a survey of UK call centres.

Company name	Type of company	Rating out of 5	Time waiting	Typical response
First Direct	24-hour telephone bank	5 star rating	No waiting time	Textbook example of a system designed for its customers
BT Cellnet	Telecoms	4 star rating	No waiting time	Simple computerised system was positive and straightforward, and used voice recognition well
Odeon Cinemas	Entertainment	2 star rating	Initially no waiting time	Long-winded computer-generated system then takes over
BSkyB	Telecoms	Nil rating	Caller asked to "please bear with us"	One option took 90 seconds before even the hold music started.
American Express	Banking	Minus rating	Minimum 5 minutes to speak to a real person	Tape says "We are currently experiencing a higher number of calls than usual – your call is important to us" – every call gets this response

THE WEB AND CRM

E-marketing isn't doing much better than bricks and mortar companies in providing decent customer service and response. In a recent survey, 150 UK companies which use an Internet address in their advertising were e-mailed with an urgent request from a potential customer. One in seven replied in 24 hours, but 39% never replied at all.

And yet, according to research conducted by McKinsey amongst members of the Chartered Institute of Marketing in 1999, consumer understanding is a key issue for 81% of marketers. E-commerce "makes for a much wider audience and a far wider range of products". It also makes customers more demanding. Customers want delivery at a specified time, just as they do with an engineer coming to service an appliance.

But there's no point in investing time, effort, and money in technological solutions to customer care problems without having the strategy and structure in place to follow up enquiries.

THE OPUS GROUP SURVEY

The Opus Group conducted a survey of Websites and discovered the following:

- 35% of Websites we surveyed had no obvious enquirer registration form.
- 46% of sites where we registered simply ignored the request for information.
- 20% of the sites where we registered acknowledged our request by e-mail and then failed to send us the information.
- 85% of the information packs received had no covering letter or method to progress the sales dialogue.
- 95% of the companies contacted failed to follow up their initial response.

And yet, the possibilities of customer care over the Internet are enormous, and undoubtedly, still in their infancy. The growing trend to conduct customer service and business via the Internet is being driven by a combination of cost, convenience and consumer demand. Put simply, it is estimated that it costs a bank about 65p per transaction in a brick and mortar outlet, 32p per telephone transaction, and 2–5p per Internet – or clicks and mortar – transaction. Companies can pass these savings on to consumers, who can browse away to their heart's content 24 hours a day.

E-business, or e-tail, can make use of a wide range of technological facilities. Consumer participation is the current trend in service delivery. Encouraging customers to participate in the service they receive allows the company or service provider to make real-time alterations on the service quality during the transaction. The Internet is the best available medium for recording and responding to consumer participation, and linked to a call centre, can provide the following benefits:

1. The Customer contact centre: The evolution of the call centre to build relationships with its customers using the telephone, the Internet, fax, e-mail, interactive TV and video conferencing in a consistent manner.
2. Internet call back: Allows a customer to request a telephone call from a human agent, at a particular time on a particular number, by clicking on a button on the company's Internet site. This request is added to a queue of similar requests at the call centre.
3. Internet chat: Allows a customer to request an immediate, interactive written exchange with someone in the call centre.
4. Voice over the Net (VON): An audio conversation with a human call centre agent. Internet technology transmits the voice and the Internet pages down the same telephone lines.

5. Video over the Net: A video conference with a human agent. The request is connected to an available agent with a video camera positioned on their terminal. A video box appears on the screens of both customer and agent so they can talk face-to-face.

6. E-mail queuing: Requests made via e-mail are added to the agent's list of things to do and are dealt with in turn.

7. Context transfer: When requests are made the call centre is shown the Web pages that the customer is using. This allows the agent to offer accurate help.

8. Intelligent AutoAgent: E-mail requests are automatically "read" by an autoagent system that can either reply to the e-mail or pass it on to the appropriate person.

Yet, with all these possibilities, there are still too few companies using technology on their Websites effectively to maximise the customer service that they can offer.

> *Example*: Dell's Website has been widely praised for its ease of use and user friendliness. They use the Website to separate business from general customers. Customers can specify the machine they are looking for and receive a price online. The call-back system can specify that you want to be called; and when.

But, some reassuring news for companies who haven't yet cracked the Internet customer service problem is that Internet demand is still in its infancy. There's still time to get it right – just. Only 13% of the UK population currently has access to the Internet at home.

Some of the UK's youngest and most dynamic companies, known for their strong Internet presence, are still doing most of their business via the phone, not the Web. First Direct – who came top in our rating of call centres – only do approximately 12% of their transactions via the Web. Egg, heralded as one of the most innovative developments in British banking over the last ten years, conducts nearly 95% of business via the phone, not the Web.

It would appear that it's not too late for companies to get it right. Shopping online is not yet widespread enough for customer service failures over the Web to have a catastrophic impact on companies attempting to do business online. But there is no doubt that it will do very soon.

CASE STUDY: CABLE AND WIRELESS

In 1997, Cable and Wireless launched in the UK with a consumer campaign focusing on customer care. By asking the question, "What can we do for you?" the campaign ushered in a whole new era for the cable TV and telecommunications sector.

The £50 million campaign was all about establishing and maintaining a dialogue between the company and its customers. Cable and Wireless conducted a survey of 1.5 million homes, asking, "What can we do for you?" – making service appear more personal at a local level. Donations to Barnardo's with every form completed provided an incentive to return questionnaires, and the campaign evolved around customer responses.

As they made clear, within our current confused and changing multimedia environment it is the companies who get their customer care message across most clearly that will survive.

Call centres and Websites are not the ultimate answer to experience marketing: in fact, they can provide a negative experience of a company, because of slow response times or poor structures and systems. Cable and Wireless made the point at their launch that "We're using the most sophisticated communications technology known to man. Our ears." Relationships are about communication, listening and talking, and listening again. If we spend too much time talking *at* our customers, whether directly, on the telephone or through advertising or direct marketing (DM), we'll fail to hear what they are saying back to us. And failure to communicate is always the fault of the transmitter – the person attempting to perform that communication. Communicate is THE central issue in Customer Relationship Management.

COMMUNICATIONS

Customer Relationship Marketers can only do their best. As Sir John Egan (BAA) pointed out, you can never totally satisfy customers. They want maximum value for the minimum price: "You have to do what you can to make profit in between." George Bull (Sainsbury) echoed this when he said, "Go for loyal customers, but lose customers who give no return." Developing and building relationships with our customers maximises customer retention, provides a better understanding of what they want and need, and leads to better profitability.

One issue is that, more than ever before, consumers are chameleons – they don't fit neatly into social demographic strata. Take an affluent customer in an upmarket area, with a good job, for instance, and you may find that on business they may fly first class and dine in excellent restaurants, but on Saturdays they may take the kids to McDonalds and have a beer in their local pub. They may fly economy on family holidays. This demonstrates the increasing difficulties with using demographic analysis to predict habits and define markets.

But we're trying to communicate in an environment that is full of background noise and full of confusion. It's a fight for attention out there, and the background noise is making life difficult for everyone.

What makes up this background noise? Competition, distraction, other pressures, different ways of working, excessive media, too much choice – these factors all make customers more and more likely to "flit" away. Customer knowledge provides companies with a competitive lead: knowing what your customers want, why they are defecting, where they are going. What's important is using and managing customer information in a blurred and confused world. Yet this isn't happening. According to research by the SAS Institute, "90% of respondents do not have entirely integrated information on their customers".

So, what sort of things should we be asking ourselves? And what are the benchmarks?

1. Who are our customers?
2. Who are the most profitable customers? What is their lifetime value?
3. How many customers are we losing, and why?
4. What value do your customers see in your products and services?
5. What are the best product and service offerings for specific customer segments?

BENCHMARKS

During an Ernst and Young/CIM debate in 1999, the following companies were asked what benchmarks they used to measure customer satisfaction. Answers were as follows:

Lloyds TBS (Michael Fairey)	Share of wallet, financial holdings, customer service (staff targets)
Sainsbury	Foot fall, loyalty card usage
BA (Lord Marshall)	Customer service, loyalty (%)
BAA (John Egan)	Return based on differential service, business fast-track usage, customer surveys, customer service

A 5% increase in customer retention for a range of service businesses estimated yield improvements in profitability from 20–85%. It is well-known that existing customers are up to seven times cheaper to retain than new customers are to acquire.

Keeping hold of your customers throughout their purchasing life seems obvious, but I would suggest that very few organisations effectively measure the economic value of their customer retention strategies.

CRM is about more than just stakeholding, relationship marketing or building consumer trust. It should encompass a whole future corporate strategy: what a company is for and how its brand equity is built and maintained.

KEY TASKS IN CRM

It is clearly necessary to establish a relationship with our customers. This should involve jointly agreeing what expectations and attributes are required if the relationship is to flourish and bring increased benefits to both parties. Softer benefits are also needed from companies, values such as empathy, confidence, and trust, as well as hard outcomes.

We need to understand that relationship management is not just about technology – it is about knowing our customers; knowing them in the past and in the future, who they are, what they want and expect, and what they are likely to want and expect in the future.

Customer focus should be at the heart of corporate strategy. Customers don't use the same language that marketers use. They don't perceive themselves as having "relationships" with companies. Their interpretation of "relationships" is understood through decent customer service, effective complaints-handling, the quality of the reception they get when they contact us by phone or in person. We need to ensure that we treat our customers as partners, not as targets. IT developments are no good without a clear customer strategy that comes from the heart of the organisation and reaches all the way through it.

We need to invest in understanding customer preferences for interactions and experiences. This helps to identify unspoken needs and create different, sometimes unexpectedly beneficial, experiences.

We need to see a move towards transparent marketing – where we as marketers are prepared to let the customer call the shots, along with a better integration of relationship marketing and marketing measurement. An integrated customer feedback system is required – and one that must result in action.

We need to remember what marketing is and what it means. As we identified earlier, "Marketing is the management process responsible for identifying, anticipating and satisfying customer requirements profitably."

In order to identify, anticipate and satisfy those requirements, we need to enter into a relationship with our customers: a relationship which is supported by technology, not dictated by it, a relationship which accommodates consumer preferences and does not expect consumers to accommodate us.

But, the simple truth is that CRM projects will spill out enormous amounts of customer data. Too many companies believe that all they have to do is collect this data and they will be able to meet cross-selling objectives. Even the big companies get it wrong. There is often no consistency in advertising from one company to the next. Companies don't use their data, except perhaps to hold the office door open. Having explored the impact of relationship management, let's now define the role.

THE ROLE

1. Preparing and executing the strategy for managing the customer, in relation to company strategy and marketing plan.

2. Creating linked tactical and creative one-to-one promotions for the Web (CRM) and offline (CRM).

3. Ensuring that there is inter-departmental buy-in to the strategy.

4. Analysing data to ensure the customer is satisfied.

5. Interpreting sales data to monitor effectiveness of product performance on- and offline.

6. Using data to target clusters of customers, identifying tactical opportunities.

7. Linking with rest of marketing team to develop tactical direct marketing and "e" campaigns in sync with other media activity.

8. Designing campaign materials with buy-in from rest of team.

9. Researching campaign and materials to assess potential impact on customers.

10. Identifying uptake from consumers.

11. Researching customers – CRM activity.

STRATEGIC FIT – TYPICAL STAKEHOLDERS AND CUSTOMERS OF JOB HOLDER

Stakeholders

1) IT department

2) CEO and board

3) Sales director and sales team

4) Customer service department

5) Marketing department

6) Administration department

7) Call centres

Customers

1) Brand managers

2) Sales managers

3) The consumer

Suppliers

1) Communication agency

2) DM agency

3) creatives

CORE COMPETENCIES

1. Developing strategy and auditing.

2. Marketing planning, segmentation and mix.

3. Marketing research skills and intelligence gathering.

4. Campaign planning.

5. Thorough understanding of e-CRM, Web technology and relevant IT tools.

6. Statistical analysis and mathematics.

7. Customer psychology.

8. Soft skills – managing stakeholders.

9. Project management skills – identifying milestones and delivery of promotions.

10. Budgeting and financial management.

NEED TO REMEMBER

1. Don't compete solely on price, especially on the Web. Create points of difference that the customer will value.

2. Don't assume that loyalty programmes will build long-term loyalty on- or offline.

3. All messages must be consistent with the brand image, to build loyalty and trust in the Brand.

4. Must be aware of ability of the best database (CRM) IT and e-CRM packages, and keep pace with technology. The best technology may not be best for your needs.

5. Manage the customer properly, and focus on the customers that generate the most revenue.

6. Deliver the message to all shareholders and achieve buy-in to plans.

7. Measure and monitor activity. Develop sensible benchmarks.

8. Ensure activity is linked to other activity and co-ordinated.

9. Only build relationships that are relevant to, and wanted by the customer; nobody wants to be spammed, junk marketed, or over committed to.

10. Don't collect irrelevant data.

SUMMARY

1. The Customer Relationship Marketer needs to take a holistic view across the product range and brands and, if appropriate, use CRM technology online and offline to manage the relationship with key customers (the ones who drive the profit), bearing in mind that:

   a) the customer is a key stakeholder

   b) it is 5–7 times cheaper to retain a customer than it is to find a new one.

2. Loyalty cards are a promotional opportunity. Affinity promotions don't buy loyalty. This comes from trust in the brand.

3. Software and hardware are techno fixes, not a substitute for marketing. Do not churn out data for the sake of it.

4. Brand building is inextricably linked with customer retention.

5. CRM software is not for everyone. Managing customer relationships is.

6. Pay special attention to the most valuable customers.

7. Obtain buy-in from the whole company and all stakeholders, especially IT and the customer service department, and call centres.

8. Be honest and fair in all dealings.

9. Whatever you do, customers will defect. Make sure it's the bad ones.

10. Standards of Web service are currently appalling.

GIVE A MARKETER THE MATRIX ROLE OF MANAGING CUSTOMER RELATIONSHIPS, AND ENSURE THEY COMMUNICATE WITH THE STAKE-HOLDERS, AND CHAMPION THE PROFITABLE CUSTOMER AT ALL TIMES.

USEFUL SOURCES

Bhote, K. (1999) "Beyond Customer Satisfaction to Customer Loyalty", Softworld Sales and Marketing Annual Survey 1999.

Foss, B. and Stone, M. (2001) *Successful Customer Relationship Marketing*, Kogan Page.

Marketing Forum Research Report (UK) (1999) Richmond Events Ltd.

Marketing Forum Research Report (1998) Richmond Events Ltd.

Reicheld, F. (2000) "E-Customer Loyalty – Applying the Traditional Rules of Business for Online Success", *European Business Journal*, **Vol 12**, 4.

Reicheld, F. (July 2000) " E-Loyalty: Your Secret Weapon On the Web", *Harvard Business Review*.

Reicheld, F. (March 1996) "Learning from Customer Defections", *Harvard Business Review*.

Shaw, R. (1998) Business Intelligence Report, "Measuring and Valuing Relationships", Thyfault.

Software Sales and Marketing (1999) Annual Survey, Imark Communications.

The Opus Group, Survey of Websites, Campaign 16 July 1999. See www.opusgroup.co.uk

TRAINING

www.cim.co.uk

www.mbs.ac.uk – Manchester Business School – CRM Masterclass

HELPFUL WEBSITES

Search CRM.com (search engine) – searchcrm.techtarget.com/

American CRM Directory – www.american-crm-directory.com

AMR Research – www.amrresearch.com/

Bain & Company – www.bain.com

CRM Community – www.crmcommunity.com/

CRM Daily – www.crmdaily.com

CRM Forum – www.crm-forum.com/

The CRM Value Chain (Professor Francis Buttle, 2000) – www.crm-forum.com/academy/cvc/cvc/pdf

CRM Gurus – www.crmguru.com/

Customer Relationship Management – www.crmproject.com/crm/home.html

Customer Contact World – www.ccworldnet.com/

Destination CRM – www.destinationcrm.com/

Direct Mail information service – www.dmis.co.uk/

European Centre for Customer Strategies – www.eccs.uk.com/

Definitions of customer relationship marketing and management – www.eccs.uk.com/resources/define.asp

eCRM Guide – www.ercmguide.com

Forrester Research – www.forrester.com/Home/0,3257,1,FF.html

Hewson-CRM software suppliers – www.hewson.co.uk

MBO – www.mbo.co.uk/

McKinsey Consultancy – www.mckinsey.com

Meta – www.metagroup.com

CRM News of Moreover.com – www.moreover.com

Opus Group – www.opusgroup.co.uk

Dr Robert Shaw – Definitions of CRM, and measuring and valuing customer relationships – www.shaw-wethey.com/html/ crm definitions. htm

Softworld – www.softworld.com/index.html

Gartner Research – www3.gartner.com/Init

THE MEDIA
MARKETER

THE MEDIA MARKETER

T his chapter considers the importance of having a marketer responsible for media. In the old, twentieth-century model, the marketing director would have overall responsibility for media, with product managers involved in each specific product or brand. The need for a manager to take responsibility across brands has occurred for the following reasons:

- There is more proliferation of media than ever before – terrestrial and satellite TV, digital TV, iTV/Web TV, direct selling activity, direct mail, e-mail, WAP phones, and magazines, cinema posters, media, digital radio. There is a profusion of channels, platforms and other media, and even a recent revival in door-to-door campaigns.
- Opportunities abound for promotion, PR and sponsorship on the plethora of new TV channels and Websites, not to mention partnership deals.

- Whilst brand managers can't take a view across the brand, the marketing director is generally too busy to take a view across these media platforms.
- No agency in the UK, or anywhere, is capable of being an expert across all these media, no matter what they tell you. Therefore, someone has to manage a roster of agencies and relationships.

We will consider the key issues that the media marketer needs to consider in developing a media strategy in consultation with the marketing director and other brand managers. We will then look at the core demographics changes that are influencing the new proliferation of media, and the current scenario for media marketers. We will then consider the problems and critical factors, and focus on the need for multi-platform mixed media comparisons. The impact of the Internet and the connected economy leads to a discussion on the key technological issues of convergence, video on demand, personal video records and broadband. Finally, we consider the measurement of effectiveness in relation to this role and draw up a job description for this matrix manager.

KEY ISSUES

The proliferation of media leads to a need for:

1. Measurement of campaign effectiveness on chosen media channels.
2. The need to contrast the effectiveness of all media, including Web activity, across brand campaigns.

This clearly requires, analytical, creative, and ingenious media planning skills.

Where to advertise, when to advertise and the choice of media mix to use are likely to have an even greater impact on advertising efficiency. These can be seen as the key "levers" of advertising efficiency that must be set by the decision-makers.

Top 20 Issues in Media

Listed below are some of the questions that the media marketer may face from his stakeholders and the other brand managers (source: Billetts Agency).

1. How can we support a diverse range of products on a limited advertising budget?
2. What is the most effective way of running a media test?
3. How can we compare investment in door drops with investment in TV advertising?
4. What is the real value of TV sponsorship relative to TV advertising?
5. What effect will the BBC1's more commercial approach to scheduling have on ITV and the commercial sector in general?
6. What action should advertisers take in response to the BBC's more commercial approach to programme scheduling?
7. What are your forecasts for TV advertisement revenue and impacts for 2001?
8. How will the management succession at Channel 5 affect their programme schedule?
9. What further sales house consolidations are likely in the next 1–2 years? If the industry consolidates, and their buying power increases, how will this affect the cost of TV media from the marketer's perspective?

10. How should I organise my online media planning and buying? Via an existing offline agency or specialist online agency?

11. How can I get accurate audience and profile figures in my online media buying?

12. How can we keep our brand at the top of consumers' minds during months when TV media is at its most expensive?

13. If advertising doesn't generate enough incremental sales to cover the cost of the media, should we advertise at all?

14. Which titles are the big cover price discounters?

15. Customer magazines, such as those of Sainsbury's and Sky, have the largest circulations, but how can we be sure that there is a reader demand for them?

16. Do national newspapers sell advertising space on their Websites separately from space in their traditional papers, or as one package? If sold separately, which will be cheaper in the long run?

17. What impact will the convergence of ownership of TV channels and software providers (e.g. Vivendi/Segram Universal) have on the global advertising marketplace?

18. Do the benefits of centralisation of media buying into international networks outweigh those of a market by market solution?

19. Can pan European media ever really compete for local budgets, or will they continue to need help from international marketing departments?

20. Should I advertise when sales are high or when costs are low?

Between 1995 and 1999 (1), UK advertising expenditure has increased from £4.8 billion to £7.2 billion; a massive increase of 50% and well ahead of RPI. The combination of a buoyant economy and expanding non-government business categories has been very good news for the advertising industry. The possible emergence of an advertising recession in 1998 and 1999 failed to occur, due to the wastefully poor marketing activity of the dot.com start ups. It is my view that the lack of professionalism shown by the dot.com companies was only exceeded by the lack of professionalism shown by the advertising profession in taking their money.

THE DEMOGRAPHIC BACKGROUND TO TODAY'S MEDIA BUYING ENVIRONMENT

Demographics: According to BMRB–TGI research:

1. **Growth** – there are 5.3 million more adults than thirty years ago.
2. **More professionals** – whilst thirty years ago, one-third were in professional occupations, today, two-thirds are in professional occupations.
3. **Better training** – thirty years ago, 12% went to university, today 25% go to university, and the Labour government in 2001, predicted that by 2005 50% will go to university. However, since 13% of the population is illiterate, we are clearly going to have some highly untrained shop assistants.
4. **End of the traditional family unit** – two-thirds of the population have no children living at home. Twenty-two per cent of housing stock is taken up by single adults.
5. **More home owners** – major increase in home ownership. More part-time working (especially amongst women).
6. **More affluence** – seventy-six per cent of adults have access to a car, while over one-third of adults have two or more cars.
7. **Fragmented buying** – changes in media consumption patterns, as we all become more "individual".
8. **Plethora of media consumed** – ITV viewing has halved. Increase in

channels has provided advertisers with an increase in commercial viewing. With increased mobility and a greater range of formats, outdoor audiences have increased. Cinema has made a spectacular recovery with reach matching the all-time highs of the 1970s.

9. **And More Of It** – in thirty years, commercial TV viewing has doubled. Weekly listening to commercial radio has doubled.

10. **Decline of newspapers** – there are 12 million fewer readers than there were twenty years ago. Sixty per cent of people read a paper today (75% in 1980).

11. **Growth of the Internet** – one-third of all UK adults now have Internet access.

12. **Lifestyle changes: Cars** – we are spending more time awake and are "sub-contracting" some of the more mundane aspects of everyday life; less time is spent preparing food, or doing household chores. It is no surprise that media owners are cashing in on this new surfeit of leisure time; on TV alone, consumer spend is up £80 compared to ten years ago.

13. **Magazines decline** – magazine readership is down 30% on twenty years ago. In fact, over the last thirty years, magazine readerships have fallen substantially, but in the last ten years, has shown signs of recovery as the market offers a greater variety of publications to reach detailed and specific target audiences.

14. **Rise of the digital viewer** – the digital viewer is younger, up-market, with a family and children. They seem to be viewing at the expense of the BBC.

15. **Critical audience** – enjoyment of TV ads has declined; they are seen as being less "novel". There is also a growing expectation that TV should keep people informed. Having said that, 50% of people in the UK are happy with the channels that they have.

Figure 3.1 shows what consumers spend each year on media.

Consumers annual spend per head on media (£ per year)

Medium	1990	2000	£ change
TV	42	122	+80
National newspapers	36	46	+10
Regional newspapers	14	15	+1
Consumer magazines	17	39	+22
Cinema	5	14	+9
Internet	0	4	+4
Total	113	239	+116

Figure 3.1   What consumers are buying into now. Source: Presentation by CIA MediaLab, July 2000

The latest figures show the growing importance of satellite and digital TV (especially in relation to sports-focused channels), and the rise in Internet use and cinema-going over the last ten years. The other figures are only keeping up with inflation.

Current Situation for Media Marketers

CIA Billetts believe that in the old model most mid-market and blue chip advertisers, chose TV companies for advertising, and then considered how to spend the balance. In new media planning, there is no point in concentrating solely on TV advertising; it has to be a totally integrated campaign across all media, from the start.

Problems for Media Marketers

Within a media environment that should solicit more experimentation, the advertiser community is relatively unprepared to change their approach. Pre-testing for media other than TV is still the exception, with measurement of effectiveness after the event similarly far more common for TV than other media. Many advertisers feel that their agencies do not always provide best advice. These same advertisers rank better targeting (through fragmented media), cost effectiveness and the development of new media as their priorities for the next five years. So the challenge is laid for advertising agencies to prove their worth.

In addition, advertisers are calling for greater transparency of agency margins, with performance-related pay and for agencies to learn more about their clients' businesses. Only 44% per cent of clients in research conducted by De Saulles Associates said that the service they received from advertising agencies was "OK". At the same time, eight out of ten believe that service was an important differentiator. Finally, only 17% believe that current fee practices are satisfactory. Is it any wonder that clients change their agencies so regularly?

The challenge for the media marketer is to measure both the effectiveness of the creative element and the efficiency of the media campaign prepared by agencies. Agencies will measure TVR (TV Ratings Point)'s impacts, gross rating points, opportunities to see, and so on.

The media marketer needs to measure:

- the impact of the message – through qualitative research before and after the campaign.
- Resultant sales compared to those from a previous campaign. Agencies' bonus payment should be linked to client sales.

Critical Factors for Media Marketers

The key factors the media market needs to bear in mind are:

- Fragmentation of audiences – there is more media out there. There is an explosion in the number and type of new media available.
- There is a trend towards mergers in media owners leading to a consolidation of agency groups/media buyers.
- There is difficulty in finding valid research. However, direct response and Web measurement is very accurate.
- They need to impact target audiences through fragmentation and diversification with the ultimate being targeting one-to-one media. Advertisers therefore, need to decide whether to make campaigns single media or multimedia.
- Tailormade advertising research shows that zapping is increasing, and ad recall varies by spot lengths. In addition advertising recall is affected by clutter – there is 28% recall swing across the break. Similarly, there can be up to a 50% swing in advertising effectiveness across programme genre. So whether the agency hits its ratings target is one thing. Whether the message sinks in to the correct audience and converts them to new products is another matter.
- According to experts, there is likely to be a reduction in the total viewing of advertisements in the UK of at least 10% by the end of the next BARB contract, and possibly by more than 30% by 2008.
- For the first time, broadband gives advertisers control over output and production.
- Advertisers have to tackle the new, two-tier consumer media society – the TV multi channel "haves" and terrestrial channel "have nots", the new techno "haves" and the traditional "have nots".

- Consumers can become "editors" and advertisers can become "media owners".
- Societe Europeenne des Satellites (SES) figures for mid-1999 show the number of digital satellite-receiving homes more than doubling in the past year – from 2.5 million to 5.5. million. Between 40% and 60% of the current SES survey of 167 million TV homes will have gone digital by 31 December 2006. By 31 December 2008, this will have increased to between 60% and 80%.

MIXED MEDIA CAMPAIGNS

There is a growing body of evidence supporting the benefits of multimedia over single media. Advertising has become much more akin to strategy than just communication. No single agency can manage this effectively. The media marketer has to implement this strategy. These are the factors to consider:

- As audiences fragment and move around, so the **environment** in which the advertisement appears becomes a major factor in advertising impact.
- Creative solutions have to be **media neutral**. Media planning used to be about optimising individual media. Today, it's all about establishing the best combination of media. Agency impartiality in media selection is under the microscope. Mixed-media planning will be the norm.
- Original research conducted with both UK and US advertisers on different attitudes to pre-testing and valuation by media has demonstrated that **each medium should be of equal worth** at the planning stage. Advertising pre-testing will not be appropriate for everyone. But it is no good investing in multimedia if we treat each medium as of different worth before we start.

Campaign effectiveness can only be optimised with the best available advertisements for each medium, otherwise we can't make media work.

- More empirical **measurement** and post-campaign **evaluation** is necessary. Tailormade empirical measurements of the return on the advertising investment go hand-in-hand with greater multimedia and advertiser-specific research.
- **Short-term-ism** has to be challenged, both in campaign planning and evaluation. It leads to poor decisions, compromised plans and damages brand equity. Short-term-ism can come from both the advertising agency – turning a slow-burn brand into a fast buck, or from the company attempting to prop up bad results with quick sales.
- Of all the new media opportunities, **interactivity** is the one that goes further in the maze, involving the consumer and providing a feedback loop.
- The **brand** has never been important. Thinking about the worth of your brand values will help chart the way through the media maze.

CIA Billetts summarise the demise of the single media and rise of the mixed media campaign as follows. The demise of single-media campaigns:

- takes much longer to reach customers
- will be noticed by a reduced number of customers
- focuses on one message
- leads to bland targeting or inappropriate targeting
- halts excess frequency and wastage.

The increase of mixed-media campaigns:

- leads to immediate high coverage levels
- leads to exposure to more potential customers

- changes emphasis on **brand** message
- leads to tighter, more effective targeting
- is a media-multiplier.

THE IMPACT OF DIGITAL/THE INTERNET

Without doubt, the adoption of digital media (TV, radio and Internet) has been a huge technological change in the late twentieth and early twenty-first centuries. Digital channels are now undermining conventional commercial viewers.

There is an expectation that Web content should be free because it was given away to start with. In the 1960s TV viewers would not have "paid per view"; it has taken 40 years to turn that perception around. However, that does not stop the potential for advertising on the Web which, if you have the right partners, can be highly beneficial.

NEW TECHNOLOGICAL ISSUES

Media Marketers need to know about new technological issues; discussed in the following sections.

Convergence in the Connected Economy

This offers three challenges to the advertising industry: other applications besides conventional broadcast entertainment will compete directly for occupation of the TV screen. Viewers will be much better able to programme their own television entertainment through interactive applications, with little effort. In addition, convergence will promote the evolution of television as a transactional medium. But, at the moment, the PC is still very much a product for the professional classes and, as such, the majority of homes do not own one. They will in the future.

Video on Demand (VOD)

The initial emphasis of VOD applications is likely to be on selling films, but it could be used to offer all forms of TV entertainment when the public wants it – news, weather, soaps, and so on. (See HomeChoice – TV when you want to watch it.) These will become like video games and the Internet will become yet another rival attraction to standard TV viewing with spot advertising.

Personal Video Records (PVR)

The PVR makes the viewer a time lord over broadcast television with the power to watch anything. . . If the telephone rings and the viewer wants to answer it, he/she can simply pause the programme and return later. Or skip the boring bits. Or maybe even (one day) delete the ads. Will enable "free" television. Could anything score higher for quality, value and convenience?

Sooner or later the introduction of the PVR will make it possible for viewers to watch broadcasts without adverts . . . advertisers and their partners should promote the concept that viewers must pay to watch PVR programming if they choose not to let the recorded commercials run.

Key options for media marketers will be to move monies into other media and/or to seek a more integrated presence through programme sponsorship. Advertisers must take seriously the audience measurement research challenge.

Broadband

Heralding a new age in electronic one-to-one communication, broadband offers the advertiser opportunities to delivery personal editorial content via the Internet without the need for a third-party media owner. Forrester Research forecasts that 36% of total European homes will have broadband connectivity by the end of 2005.

Broadband is the prize: the power, authority and entertainment of television combined with the interactive and non-linear functionality of the Internet. It is currently accessible to about 400,000 homes across Europe, with Sweden, Germany and the Netherlands being the most advanced markets.

From the consumer's perspective, an "always-on" connection will make it quick and easy to access the Internet, any television channel and any radio station and, crucially, all the new broadband sites/channels whenever they want. At the same time, for advertisers, broadband will create profound changes in the relationship they have with increasingly sophisticated and global market consumers. The critical emotional relationships between consumers and a brand's provenance will be forged electronically through broadband interactivity, with a sophistication and personalisation far beyond the 30″ commercial.

Content is therefore going to become even more important in a broadband world. Surfers will flock to sites that carry original and entertaining videos as opposed to still pictures and text, and similarly to interactive digital TV channels that are relevant and exciting.

Creative marketers could see broadband as the mechanism with which to create and develop involving and long-term relationships with their consumers. However, it is unlikely that this will be the preserve of the traditional advertising agency.

Smart companies are going to need new forms of help to progress the development of their brand channels. Advertising agencies will struggle to get it because the work required is too much of a daily editorial grind and probably not remunerative enough.

MEASURING EFFECTIVENESS

We need to reconsider why we advertise in the first place. The generally accepted core reasons are as follows:

1. Generate incremental sales, especially in direct advertising.
2. Generate Return on Investment (ROI) possibly in brand equity.
3. Reinforce category leadership, possibly also as a barrier to entry.
4. Underwrite future profitability, possibly by building short-term brand share.

Twenty years ago most companies measured effectiveness by how many boxes left the factory. Today, there needs to be a more "holistic" approach. We need to evaluate both long-term effectiveness and the short-term effect. Whatever the ultimate objective of advertising, the advertiser should have a clear view of how ROI is going to be delivered in order to maximise advertising effectiveness.

Ultimately, effectiveness, whilst partly about building brands, must deliver profit – not TVRs, eyeballs, or any other measure. Advertising efficiency can be defined as the ratio between advertising payback and cost.

RELATIONSHIPS BETWEEN CLIENTS AND AGENCIES

Clients must become more "media savvy" – often dealing direct with agency planners, rather than account managers, as well as juggling the inputs of smaller, more specialist agencies focused on fragmented media channels.

It is easy for agencies to hide behind the "old chestnut" of immeasurability. Payment by results is necessary. Clients accuse agencies of using a "smoke and mirror" approach, but since agencies say clients fail to understand key issues, a compromise is required.

Payment by results (PBR) is not an easy approach. It is often accused of failing to include the contribution of advertising to overall company performance and share price, or take into account agency service levels. Another issue is, how do you measure subtle changes in brand awareness? Despite these difficulties, PBR is expected to account for between 75% and 90% of all US ad agency agreements by 2005.

TYPICAL AGENCY METRICS

1. *TV*

Impacts – total audience (doesn't mean it actually had any impact on them at all).

Frequency – opportunities to see the ad (based on programmes watched by the sample, but doesn't deduct those who make a cup of tea in the break).

TV Rating – the average percentage of potential audience who saw the ad (can be based on small and in unrepresentative samples and needs to be recalibrated so you can compare, say, Sky with GMTV – increasingly it is impossible to accurately measure success on small audience satellite or digital channels).

Most metrics can be fiddled by building impacts with ten-second ads. The best approach is to find a way of linking sales directly to ads, with, say, a two week gap between screening and purchase (avoid agencies that win awards, they don't usually sell products).

2. *Magazines*

"Readership" makes the dubious assumption that people pass the publication around: they could equally put it straight in the bin. Also make sure the circulation isn't boosted by freebie giveaways to impress advertisers.

Psychologists would say always go for a left hand page near the front of a magazine to gain maximum impact, and avoid the classified section.

3. *PR*

Be aware of the following:

Column inches – it's not how long it is, it's what it says.
Circulation – Free sheets have a huge circulation, but will they be read?
Metrics – electronic tools exist e.g. by subscribing to Reuters or Media Disk, but you could also subscribe to Reuters, for instance, and track your own articles. You should build your own system of awarding points for:

- being positive
- being on-strategy – giving the correct message
- position – front page better than inside
- dedicated headings
- relevant pictures
- the importance of the publication to your target market.

An exemplary article meeting all the above perfectly might score 6, for instance, and could be multiplied by the circulation. Watch out for agencies that score a "teletext" article as a hit of 55 million.

4. *The Web*

Stickyness – number of visitors based on eyeballs/hits (unreliable).
Click-throughs – slightly more reliable.
Online sales – the best measure.

5. *Others*

Radio, posters, cinema and so on tend to sell "packages". Results are difficult to quantify through traditional means.

METRICS THE MEDIA MARKETER SHOULD USE

Pre-TV creative test   – Qualitative research
Post-TV campaign effectiveness – Qualitative/Quantitative research

TV and other media	– Compare with previous campaigns
Sales	– Compare with history, year-on-year
Customer survey	– What influenced purchase – survey/ telemarketing
Brand tracking	– Brand awareness, annual survey, qualitative

The biggest mistake most companies make is not building enough research budget into the overall advertising budget, thereby building campaign knowledge to effectively judge the current campaign and create a benchmark for the next one. Roughly 10% of campaign funds should be put aside for research.

THE ROLE

1. Generating effective campaigns, pan-brands in consultation with other marketers and management.

2. Building knowledge of all possible on- and offline media channels.

3. Recruiting and building relationships with a roster of agencies with specialisms in selected channels.

4. Working with media planners at agencies to develop cost-effective plans to achieve brand strategies.

5. Monitoring agency "actuals" versus plan.

6. Setting up appropriate qualitative and quantitative research programmes to monitor agency and campaign effectiveness, and benchmark achievements.

7. Feed back campaign analyses to stakeholders.

Stakeholders	*Customers*	*Suppliers*
CEO	Marketers	Roster agencies
Marketing directors	PR executive	Research companies
Sales team		Telesales agents

CORE COMPETENCIES

1. Statistical analysis and mathematics.

2. Negotiation skills.

3. Campaign planning.

4. Market research.

5. Creative skill awareness/lateral thinking.

6. Soft skills – managing customers and suppliers.

7. Communication skills.

SUMMARY

1. There are more media channels than ever before, which makes communication through media channels extremely complex.

2. New opportunities exist in the connected economy, success is difficult to measure, in terms of brand building, but on short-term effectiveness, sales is the key barometer.

3. The world is becoming smaller, but targeting clusters of individuals, and one-to-one marketing, places huge demand on achieving the optimum channel efficiency.

4. Companies can no longer lead on TV: campaigns have to be approached on a level playing-field basis.

5. Success depends on good measurement, monitoring, feedback, knowledge-building and benchmarking.

6. No one agency can deliver efficiently across the proliferation of media channels. The media marketer has to manage relationships across a number of agency specialists.

USEFUL SOURCES

Broadbent, S. (1989) *The Advertising Budget*, NTC.

Fraizer, G. (1994) *Advertising Effectiveness*, NTC.

Yedin, D. (1994) *Creating Effective Marketing Communications*, Kogan Page.

TRAINING

CAM courses (delivered by CIM) – Find out more at www.cim.co.uk or call +44 1628 427500.

Institute of Practitioners in Advertising (IPA) – Find out more at www.ipa.co.uk

Institute of Public Relations (IPR) – Find out more at www.ipr.co.uk

HELPFUL WEBSITES

Eurowireless forum – www.212.53.86.122/eurowireless

Mobile Wireless forum – www.mwif.org

UK WAP group – www.thewapgroup.com

Wap forum – www.wapforum.org

Wireless Marketing Association – www.wirelessmarketing.org.uk/

LEADING COMPANIES

M-Commerce (Mobile commerce) – www.accenture.com/xd/xd.asp?it=
enweb&xd=ecommerce.mcommerce

FAQs on WAPS – www.as.corlorline.no/wap-faq/

Ericsson – www.ericsson.com/WAP/

Forrester Research – www.forrester.com/ER/Press/Release/
0,1769,400,FF.html

News on WAPS – www.moreover.com

Newsdesk – www.newsdesk.com

Nokia – www.nokia.com/corporate/wap/future.html

Orange – www.orange.co.uk

Phone.com – www.phone.com

Vodafone – www.vodafone.co.uk

Introduction to WAP technology – www.webproforum.com/wap/index/html

THE SUPPLY CHAIN MARKETER

THE SUPPLY CHAIN MARKETER

Supply Chain Management (SCM) has always been important to any business, whether in a B2B or B2C environment. This has now become even more of a focus to both manufacturing and service environments.

The discussion has focused on how is it possible to maximise value for the end consumer whilst simultaneously stripping out the cost of manufacture and process along the supply chain? The win win is to achieve an equilibrium where the customers gets what they want at a reasonable and competitive price, and the company maximises its profit because:

- resources have been used optionally
- all wastage and duplication has been stripped out of the value chain
- companies down the chain are focusing on what they do best; their core competence.

This chapter looks at the importance of SCM, giving examples of successful implementation, and discusses the importance of the role of marketing and the SC marketer in maximising a company's efficiency. The role will involve internal marketing and importing knowledge to the key stakeholders in the operations and logistic chain.

DEFINING SUPPLY CHAIN MANAGEMENT

The Global Supply Chain Management Forum defines SCM as:

> The integration of business processes from end user through original suppliers that provide products, services, and information that add value to customers.

SCM has its roots in manufacturing. In many industries suppliers and partners work together to strip out costs and improve efficiency in the supply chain for mutual benefit. They have found that to survive they have had to be more responsive and nimble on their feet, to respond swiftly to bottlenecks and share information. To achieve this, partners need to have balanced power in a co-operative venture. In the marketing context this means choosing which aspects to collaborate on, and sharing information about mutual customers and, often, integrating campaigns and activities. In this context it is not surprising to find associations between Ford and Chrysler, or Ford and Seat in Spain.

Supply chain partnerships can work across chains as well as up and down chains. A competitor on one product or market may be a partner in another. The marketer, therefore, needs to co-ordinate and communicate in each direction; as shown in Figure 4.1.

Figure 4.1   Supply chain partnerships.

ADDING VALUE

Many companies have gained, and continue to gain, competitive advantage from information technology logistics solutions. Wal-mart's distribution strategy is a good example. For them a focus on the consumer led to greater profitability.

There are two key aspects to the supply chain:

- The technology to manage the logistics.
- Building relationships and common (win-win) goals for participants in the chain.

If value can be added all through the chain, and performance improved, everyone should win, especially the consumer, since there is no added value whatsoever unless the consumer makes the purchase. It's important to remember that what is profit to the company is cost to the consumer.

In the global car market, for instance, where the average margin on cars for the producer is 2%, the more economies that can be made by outsourcing elements or sub-assemblies upstream (up the chain) to companies entirely focused on a particular aspect of the production process, the better. In the

Ford motor companies case, their focus is on developing the brand, New Product Development (NPD), and getting closer to the customer, whilst stripping costs out of the chain.

The main factor for most businesses is activity integration to create a seamless channel of delivery. In FMCG (Fast Moving (perishable) Consumer Goods), SCM best practice is often considered to be the practice of ECR (Efficient Customer Response). This requires:

- efficient stock replacement.
- the right stock in the right place to support effective marketing promotion in-store, including co-ordination of point of sale materials.
- efficient range stocking to maximise consumer take-up.
- efficient new product introduction.

Response has been improved by standardising, for instance, carton sizes, pallet sizes, load weights, barcoding, electronic data management, standard ordering procedures, invoicing and receipt of goods notices. The need to have standard definitions and control of product categories gave rise to the need to have a category-focused marketer in the retail environment, hence the Category Marketer. This has helped Wal-mart in the US, and grocers such as Tesco and Sainsbury in the UK.

To successfully minimise expensive stock holding, the technology has to link successfully through an intranet. Clearly the marketing needs to be spot-on to ensure the right stock is in the right place at the right time, and that back-up stock is available. The grocery producers or, for instance, toy manufacturers' dilemma is to balance the stock well and not have perishable products in the factory. Nobody wants toys in February, as early Internet toy vendors discovered.

The equivalent in a service industry is to match the fronted staffing levels to the promotion. Are there enough people in the call centre to manage the demand from direct advertising; can we scale the service up or down to meet the demand; and are our partners in the chain geared up for the relative demand level?

The process which can be linked by technology looks like that shown in Figure 4.2.

Estimates for savings in the grocery business in the US are $30 billion and £25 billion in Europe in the 1990s. Savings were also made in other manufacturing industries, such as cars and pharmaceuticals.

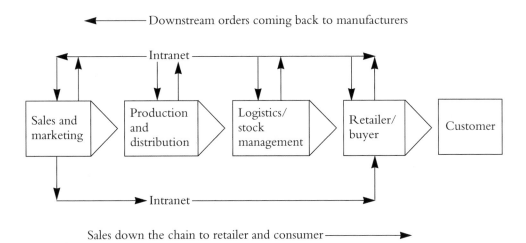

Figure 4.2 The technology-driven process to market.

CREATING VALUE THROUGH THE INTERNET (SUPPLIER INTRANETS)

The idea of intranet links down the chain implies trust and transparency between players. The focus is inevitably on minimising stock or staff levels, but with good enough support to guarantee fast turn-around when required. The intranet transfers behaviour into action, as the entire chain reacts to live purchase data, maximising the efficiency of the planning cycle in the process.

In the service scenario, viewing progress down the chain enabled FedEx to allow customers to track where their parcels were as they travelled around the world to their door. In the travel industry it allows high street travel shops to book airline tickets and holidays for consumers in real time. However, in terms of customer service, the marketer's touch is not always present. Why, for instance, is luggage at airports not scanned by barcode? Why do you have to fill in a form when they lose your luggage? Shouldn't they know what it is and where it is?

There are many examples of successfully leveraged added value, including the following:

- Body Shop use a system called SPEX to accurately speed up export documentation and process.
- General Electric use the web to schedule shipments from networked warehouses. They also reduce purchasing staff by 50% because of their intranet system.
- The Ford Motor Company use an intranet to track spare parts shipments. Typically, the US experience is that 10% to 15% of supply chains costs can be stripped out using on-line methods.
- At Cisco the entire buying process is controlled through the intranet with suppliers being asked to quote online.

Opportunities presented by the Internet include:

1. Better and easier purchasing procurement.
2. Direct ordering and scheduling – inventory management.
3. Tracking where product is in the supply chain and transportation.
4. Managing Out of Stocks (OOS) better.
5. Ability to invoice online.
6. Ability to link support information e.g. marketing promotions/campaigns, product specifications and launch dates.
7. Reduction in human element of process and cost savings down the line.
8. Ability to manage customer service and complaints handling.
9. Ability to manage the buying function.
10. Handling systems, warehousing, packaging process and returns.

The Internet has proven to be an important communication link with vendors, and has bound together the supply chain.

THE MARKETER'S PERSPECTIVE OF SCM

From a marketing perspective SCM falls into the area of internal marketing to operations-related stakeholders and, to some extent, external suppliers, partners and retailers. It is important that the supply chain understand the impact of marketing activity because:

1. It is likely to skew demand for a product or service.
2. Activity with a trade customer or vendor impacting on point of purchase will influence demand.

3. Will heavily influence the take-up of New Products (NPD) and seasonality
   of demand.

There are a number of factors involved in such internal marketing campaigns:

- Need to generate internal awareness of important activity, launches, focuses
  and strategem.
- Need to identify the information needs of the various internal stakeholders
  and communicate messages that are relevant to them, relative to their
  expectations.
- Discuss the impact of the marketing objectives to ensure they are understood and are achievable (SMART objectives, to be discussed later).
- Stakeholders in return need to plan carefully around these objectives and
  deliver within the service capabilities of the firm.
- Agree measures for internal service quality and benchmarks. A service level
  guarantee is needed.

The SC marketer must ensure that strategy, objectives and action plans are
discussed and agreed with suppliers and suppliers' marketing teams, buyers,
R&D teams, operations managers, factory or service providers, call centres, sales
teams and vendors, so that campaigns match delivery schedules and fit the
"just-in-time" (JIT) requirements of the operations management. Horror stories
abound of TV campaigns running with no stock in the retail trade, professional services direct TV campaigns with inadequate call centre staff to take the
calls, and Websites crashing at vital moments.

Key Points of Contact for SC Marketers

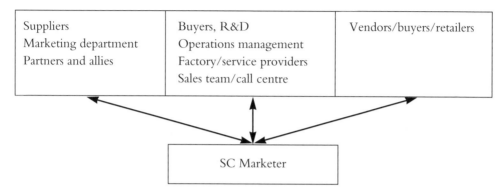

Figure 4.3   Key contacts.

Figure 4.3 shows the key points of contact for a SC marketer. To be successful the company needs to have excellent process, technology and organisational capabilities. To make the most of these attributes, the SC marketer needs to ensure that accurate and timely information is made available and input into the planning process.

Examples of necessary capabilities are:

- Maximum resource utilisation through knowledge of marketing activity.
- Demand-focused and swift scheduling to meet marketing demand.
- Customer-driven supply focus – delivering to strategically most "needy" client/customer.
- Integration with the supply chain through intranet systems to build marketing plan awareness amongst stakeholders.
- Just-in-time production that meets customer requirements with reasonable lead times in accordance with marketing plans.

- Measurement, focus and team-playing – goodwill and flexibility are required between marketing and operations functions.

Apart from campaigns, launches, and planned consumer-facing activity, the SC Marketer should be able to share research findings and information on the consumer with the retailer/vendor and back up the chain. The more that all key players understand the customer, the better the perspective of needs and focus. After all, everyone has the same objective in mind; customer profitability through customer satisfaction.

Managing and running the technology that can cluster customer information and provide knowledge up the supply chain is often farmed out by most companies to Application Service Providers (ASPs) and there are literally thousands of such organisations managing data and data warehouses. Fundamental to this activity is the belief that observing buyer behaviour can lead to the successful prediction of future buyer behaviour.

CHANNEL RELATIONSHIP BUILDING

As stated above, the SC marketer also needs to build a relationship with operations management and manage costs. Traditionally in a manufacturing SC, 50% of the costs are inventory. The focus for the marketer and operations is cost reduction, to maximise profit at a price the customer is willing to pay. Both are therefore looking to develop channel partners both on- and offline, find strategic alliances and comfortable up- and downstream alliances.

However, healthy conflict exists between the SC marketer and the operations management, as shown in Table 4.1, which needs to be managed maturely.

Table 4.1   Differences between the SC marketer and an operations manager.

SC marketer	Operations manager
Maximum profit	Maximum scale efficiency
Maximum sales units	Optimum resource utilisation
Maximum revenue	Maximum realistic mark up
Excellent customer service	Market average customer service
Regional warehousing/back-up	Large drops from central source
High inventory	Low inventory
Wide product range	Standardisation

The differences cannot be ignored. Both parties need to prescribe to, and endorse, the long-term profit-maximising position. That is to say, they must agree the most efficient process to satisfy customer needs most profitably, but should not compromise future earnings, for instance, by upsetting a valued customer. There may be a justifiable requirement to offer customised products or services; or it may be totally uneconomic to a particular partner, channel or retailer/vendor to offer a customisation service to small customers. Often, inventory SKUs (Stock Keeping Units) or production downtime is necessary to manage a small run, which would make the latter unrealistic.

Similarly, in a service environment, too much variation from standard customer-facing operations may have a negative impact on the core business and profitability.

THE ROLE

1. Awareness of intranet technology.

2. Generation and co-ordination of category action plans.

3. To collate plans from brand managers and sales activity plans and ensure relevant operations management stakeholders are aware of the planned impact on stock, people, process and distribution.

4. Liaise with partners, retailers and allies.

5. Attend production-related meetings and scheduling meetings.

6. Benchmark against competitors supply chain.

Stakeholders/Customers

Operation management
Distribution management
Customer service department
Call centre staff
Sales management
Marketers
Finance management
Purchasing department

Suppliers

Suppliers companies
(IT Vendors)
Retailers/Customers

CORE COMPETENCIES

1. Planning skills/Project-focused

2. Team player

3. Attention to detail

4. Communication skills

SUMMARY

1. SCM is becoming very important in the drive to strip out cost and add value to the supply chain. The focus is now on the customer.

2. The marketer's role in SCM is crucial, to ensure that all the players in the chain are aware of activity that will secure demand.

3. Marketers need to be aware of all the implications of strategic action e.g. it is cost-effective to keep the range as narrow as possible; creating low volume niche products drives up costs and limits flexibility.

4. Collaboration involves external as well as internal partnerships.

5. The technology is the window, but human relationships are the key to success.

6. Intranets can typically strip out 10%–15% of the channel cost by reducing human input, and removing duplicity in the process.

USEFUL SOURCES

Johnson, G. and Scholes, K. (1999) *Exploring Corporate Strategy*, Prentice Hall.

Nevan-Wright, J. A. (1999) *The Management of Service Operations*, Continuum International Publishing Group.

Wild, R. (1999) *Production and Operations Management*, third edition, Cassell.

TRAINING

www.bre.co.uk/CPIC/service2.html – Dedicated to supply chain management in the construction industry.

www.smthacker.co.uk/training supply chain.htm – Consultants specialising in supply chain management and training.

www.supply-chain-training.co.uk/index.html – Training relating to the management of the supply chain, useful for the buying side of marketing.

HELPFUL WEBSITES

www.cips.org/ – Chartered Institute of Purchase and Supply.

www.dti.gov.uk/mbp/bpgt/m9gb00001/m9gb000011.html – The UK governments Department of Trade and Industry site, which has training details.

www.mcb.co.uk/scm.htm – Own the Emerald database of management-focused content.

www.stile.coventry.ac.uk/stile/web/web supply chain.htm – Coventry Business School in the UK, with supply-chain focused section.

www.supplymanagement.co.uk – The site of the *Supply Management* magazine.

www.tvt.co.uk/scn/ – Thames Valley Technology, a UK organisation who run seminars on supply chain management.

THE KNOWLEDGE MARKETER

THE KNOWLEDGE MARKETER

Knowledge Management, or KM, must surely be on the radar screen of every marketer and every business, either because a system is being implemented in their companies, or at the very least, through literature and magazines which have found their way to the marketer's desk.

The idea that if we look at what we have done in the past, to avoid repeating mistakes, and similarly to copy the best of the past, is hardly new. What is new is that technology now gives us a convenient framework on which to hang this information and channel it in useful ways, so that we can drop in and learn from experience. The other new dimension is that online chat areas and company intranets allow thoughts and ideas to be passed around and built on. Therefore, used correctly, this is a powerful tool for New Product Development (NPD) and innovation. It allows different functions to communicate with each other in a non-linear non-time or geography-dependent manner, producing a creatively synergistic environment.

The technology is just a framework on which to place knowledge. What is also needed is a business culture that rewards contributions to the online KM system. The knowledge marketer has a crucial contribution to this because the individual with this responsibility will have to pull together the contributions from all the marketers and add these to the system. Some information will be reluctantly given because people will not want to associate themselves with a campaign that has been deemed a failure.

This chapter explores some of the benefits of knowledge management that have been experienced by leading companies in various environments, and offers guidelines for the management of knowledge. I will conclude with an analysis of the role and skills required to succeed.

AN OVERVIEW

This topic is at the heart of innovation and New Product Development (NPD) and the future for collaborative marketing. No-one wants to keep making the same mistakes as they have made in the past, and most marketers want to be progressive and dynamic. The role of knowledge marketer will help make marketers be seen as responsible corporate players, and help to achieve measurements and benchmarks of marketing activity. It is, therefore, a crucial role.

Tom Peters in his book *Thriving on Chaos* talked about a world that is becoming increasingly fast, a world where people need to take chances and learn quickly from their mistakes. The "have a go" argument is that it is better to make a lot of cheap mistakes and make some progress, than to go slow and end up making one gigantic mistake. These days people have to make decisions swiftly, and the more information they can get quickly, the more informed they will be and the better their decision will be. This, in essence, is what knowledge management information systems try to provide. There is also a need to avoid what I call marketing amnesia. Too few companies have a debrief session after launching a project, let alone store any relevant information for future use. Since a product manager's average tenure before moving on is 18 months, this is very surprising. It is little wonder that knowledge is lost.

First, we should define knowledge. Knowledge is information plus rich experience, and therefore, it is more valuable than the strings of data churned out by computers over the last fifty years.

DEFINING KNOWLEDGE MANAGEMENT (KM)

Knowledge Management or KM introduces the idea of taking knowledge and systemising it for the benefit of all users. It is defined by David Snowden (Institute of Knowledge Management) as "The identification, optimisation and active management of intellectual assets".

Hugh Wilmott comments:

KM is a slippery term. It has become widely used but lacks any unified, consistent meaning. Nonetheless, knowledge is being identified as a key asset, and changing methods and forms of work organisation are transforming the way in which knowledge is produced, shared and valued.
(Hugh Wilmott, Ch. 3 in *Knowledge Management: A Real Business Guide*)

The Academic Background

- In the 1960s Peter Drucker talked about the "knowledge society". He said in future the basic economic unit will be knowledge.

- Nonaka and Takeuchi looked at two types of knowledge, tacit and explicit, based on experience in the job (uncodified knowledge) and written process knowledge (codified). They also said that knowledge was the key asset for the future.
- More recently, Thomas Stewart believed that intellectual capital is the hidden asset that comes from knowledge. There are three types: a) human capital – managers' talent; b) customer capital – trademarks/brands, relationships, databases; and c) structural capital, such as process know-how.

The drive for knowledge management comes from the pace of change, the need to reduce supply chain costs through know-how, the growth of IT as an enabler, and the recognition of the value of the past in predicting future success of projects.

WHAT THE SURVEYS SAY

A number of surveys have been undertaken which put knowledge management into perspective. The Industrial Society claim that 87% of companies believe they are in a knowledge-based business, and point out that Skandia AFS publish an intellectual capital balance sheet in their annual report. Similarly, Dow Chemical have generated $125 million in revenue from intellectual property, and Ernst & Young in the US attribute one-quarter of the annual performance review on their employees' contribution to the knowledge process. Buckman Labs, the US multinational, measures 1200 employees' contribution to knowledge they create and knowledge they share with others.

According to a study by Ernst & Young, 96% of UK companies surveyed felt that customer knowledge was the most important asset for maintaining competitiveness, closely followed by knowledge of best practice through bench-marking, corporate competencies and capabilities, the products and services themselves, and finally market trends. Some 33% of the respondents claimed to be in the process of developing a KM system to improve their knowledge base and competencies.

A survey by the *Journal of Knowledge Management* and the Best Practice Club found that implementing KM benefits companies by improving decision-making, increasing responsiveness to customers, improving the efficiency of people and operations, leading to better products and service and greater innovation. In some cases, the culture of the company gets in the way; the system only works if it is seen to be important to the CEO and the board, and if it is recognised in the reward structure of the company. In addition, the following other problems in implementing KM were cited:

- lack of problem ownership (64%)
- lack of time (60%)
- structure (54%)
- internal commitment (46%)
- lack of rewards (46%)
- emphasis on individuals, not teamwork (45%).

In 2000, the Delphi Group surveyed 700 companies in the US, and found that 77% expected to adopt KM initiatives within two years, 53% saw it as a valu-able approach to business, and 32% saw KM as a major imperative.

Research across Europe by the Cranfield School of Management with the Fraunhofer Institute in Berlin in 1998 indicated that 85% of companies believe that restriction of information on a "need to know" basis is dying, and that, therefore, workers were happy to share information. Ninety-four per cent of respondents felt that the future would require people to share more information. Increase in spending on KM systems was predicted to grow by 70% in three years. In addition, 85% believed that knowledge assets would drive business value. However, 40% did not currently consider their companies "learning organisations". Finally, 62% believed that KM was not a fad; and we shall discuss this later on.

KNOWLEDGE MANAGEMENT AND MARKETING

We will look at KM from a marketing perspective. The system should, however, be part of a much larger whole, whereby information is brought together across the whole company with input from:-

1. IT in procuring and upgrading knowledge management systems.
2. HR in keeping internal training and staff records updated.
3. Finance, in providing and updating financial knowledge on our own company, our customers and supply chain.
4. Board, recording strategy, outcomes and benchmarks such as a balanced scorecard.
5. Marketing, sharing knowledge on competitors, markets, our products and services, benchmarks, campaign measurement and validation, market research.
6. Sales, sharing knowledge of accounts and activities to help both the manager and his customer when problems or choices occur.

At one level, the tool for KM is computer software. This is, as I have mentioned, merely a helpful platform and structure on which to store information.

Although it is necessary to purchase some basic software, what is much more important is the quality of information you store, how it is indexed and codified, who is empowered to use and update information, and how it is retrieved.

There are therefore two dimensions of KM:

1. The technology required, systems and procedures, and
2. The people, culture, attitude and focus of individuals. In other words, if the organisation doesn't "buy in" to the importance of such a system from CEO or MD downwards, it will fail.

In addition, there are two types of knowledge covered by knowledge management:

1. Implicit knowledge – of systems processes, which are often documented.
2. Tacit knowledge – things understood by people, such as rites or rituals, or cultural understanding, which is rarely written down.

In terms of the way knowledge is accumulated, the size of the company is a factor – small companies tend to function and make decisions around tacit knowledge. As companies grow, they produce formal systems and processes and focus on implicit knowledge.

Because we are all inherently lazy, this knowledge has tended to remain undocumented, but with the advent of knowledge management technology, the process has become more manageable. And, it is not just marketers who are lazy – a survey of IT directors in the mid-1990s asked what they would do to prepare for the Y2K problem. The second most common answer was – "I won't be working here then."

ISN'T KM JUST ANOTHER FAD OR BUZZWORD?

Yes it is. We have had, to name but a few:

- Scientific Management – Taylorism, Henry Ford, batch processing and so on.
- Total Quality Management (TQM)
- Business Process Re-engineering (BPR)
- Customer Relationship Management (CRM) – one to one marketing
- Knowledge Management (KM).

So isn't it all just terminology inflation?

Beneath the froth, and regardless of the fact that the "buzzness" may line the pockets of technology companies and consultants, I believe that the idea is sound. How much time, money and effort could a company save if it shed its collective amnesia regarding previous successes and failures? What is the cost of not knowing? It is the cost of:

- Reinventing the wheel
- Trying out square wheels
- Launching square wheels
- Customer disappointment with the square wheels, therefore a negative impact on the brand
- Competitors using round wheels.

A recent survey by KPMG found that only two out of 100 blue chip companies in the UK thought knowledge management was a fad.

WHY DO WE NEED IT?

Marketers need to concentrate on building knowledge through communities to hold, share, and grow knowledge. For instance, there may be good reasons why a particular campaign approach does not work, but since the average product manager stays at a company for 18 months, and agencies are changed regularly, how do you avoid making the same mistakes again and again? In this respect, a key issue is that few people can be bothered to document or create a case study from a particular product launch or activity. Ironically, there is often more to be learned from previous failures than from successes.

There are three good reasons for the marketing team to adopt a KM approach:

1. Why bother reinventing knowledge or searching for information if you have it on your own system, which will save time and effort.
2. It can be used internally for justification of an approach for marketing a new product or service, and achieve buy-in from management.
3. It sets up the image of the marketing team as a professional operation, taking on board experience and knowledge down the years. It reduces the risk of "firing from the hip".

Using this information and stored knowledge will prove to be an extremely helpful process in decision-making. Knowledge is the mother of invention. It saves time and minimises mistakes, as well as answering the questions – who can help me; who knows the solution?

In most companies, even in product manufacturers, service is increasingly important, and in service businesses the customer relationship is paramount. Therefore, adding value by understanding the customer better is crucial to bottom-line success. KM is a key way by which this marketing objective can be met.

INNOVATION

One of the main benefits of KM is its help with the innovation process. This encompasses not just NPD ideas generation, but the implementation of change to processes and actions. By giving key employees a place to store "insights" electronically as an "aide memoires", technology can help in the process. Fundamentally the system needs to offer individuals the opportunity to:

1. Share the insights of others.
2. Add their own insights and ideas.
3. Be able to data search on topics and look for relationships between seemingly unconnected facts.
4. Provide community space where people researching the same topics can communicate.

One way of sharing insights is for the company to insist that if anyone attends a training course or conference, they must prepare a paper on what they have learned and attach any course notes which can then be added to the knowledge space.

The key software required is, of course, excellent people.

COMPETITIVE ADVANTAGE

Smart companies in the twenty-first century need to keep competitive advantage by:

- sharing knowledge across borders e.g. functional, divisional, geographical,
- identifying partners to share information with, for mutual benefit,
- being open to change processes and systems,
- incentivising managers to share information, usually by linking the requirement to their reward structure,
- storing only focused information linked to strategy.

Examples of Implementation

Shell runs hundreds of online communities to support its engineers. Similar support is available to employees at BP, Accenture and Unilever for instance. Of course, the process didn't start with technology; many companies, such as Procter & Gamble, have been doing this for decades, where bulletins, communicating experiences and innovations from plants around the world, were encouraged. Managers in such companies have always been encouraged to be innovative. Managers had to follow simple routines for accessing and reporting company "library" information.

3M have created a KM database and multiple overlapping scientific networks, and have a 15% rule, where employees must spend 15% of their time on their own projects using these networks – no more, no less. They then have to generate 25% of company turnover from products that have been introduced in the last four years.

BT have had library resources for years. What technology has meant for BT is that they can now put customer experience, from the sales and marketing team, plus codified instructions for engineers, and learning materials from all staff, on an intranet, which results in easy access for employees at home offices, or from anywhere in the world.

Hewlett Packard has created a technical product called "E-sales Partner" to provide support through technical product information, sales presentations, sales and marketing tactics, customer account information, and other processes.

Nokia have created teams of "knowledge champions" to establish best practice; they encourage shared mindsets, shared visions, shared values and attitudes, and they reward knowledge sharing.

General Motors has created a system targeted to capture "learning in action" – the wisdom and experience that is used in the daily task of making decisions.

Booz Allen created a system called "Knowledge Online", which is a database and datamap of what the firm knows and who knows it. It is an education tool for consultants, a repository for standardised information on IT and methodologies, and a means of generating cutting-edge thinking amongst partners.

John Brown of BP attributes 80% of their success to the successful use of shared knowledge technology, and 20% to the technology. A director in Columbia was initially unwilling to share knowledge of how their engineering process worked, but when he needed help in putting together a process of redundancy management, he was able to call on the knowledge of the HR team's KM system. In return, knowledge of the Columbian engineering projects is now shared.

McDonalds have a sophisticated system for order processing, cooking, marketing, promoting and franchising, captured into their business process. They are able to experiment and adjust the process over time.

Ernst & Young offered a £1000 prize to the 10 staff who contributed most to knowledge sharing in order to get their system off to a flying start. This way they received around 500 contributions a month to start with, which settled down to 300 contributions a month.

In 1998 Chevron claimed that they saved $150million a year by sharing knowledge on energy use.

Texas Instruments created a virtual wafer plant by sharing knowledge and best practice with other plants. This in turn increased productivity in existing plants and saved $500 million at each plant.

Silicon Graphics reduced sales training costs by 90% using product information systems.

Hoffman La Roche, maker of Valium, saved itself from bankruptcy in 1978 by sharing R&D strategic knowledge with the biotech industry.

ICL created a global information service which is hosted on their intranet. The knowledge area is called Café Vik (which stands for Valuing ICL's Knowledge). It covers ICL knowledge, customers and partners, services and products, processes and policies, and company-wide expertise. Recruitment, induction, performance management and reward structures have recently been added.

Anglian Water Services decided to build their knowledge base through an encyclopaedia of water and by tapping (forgive the pun) into expert sources of knowledge inside the company and externally through consultants. They created a learning space to share ideas, by working with external partners.

It is surprising how many companies don't use such disciplines. It is easy to fall in the trap of being so busy running that you don't stop to check that you are running in the right direction, or that there isn't a better way of getting there.

Business Excellence

The European Foundation for Quality Management (EFQM) sees knowledge management as fundamental to business excellence, and highlights KM enablers and the impact they have on the business, as shown in Table 5.1.

Table 5.1   Knowledge management enablers and their impact.

Knowledge Management Enablers – necessary

Support to succeed
Leadership
People management
Policy and strategy
Resources
Processes

Knowledge Management Impact – results expected

Business success
People satisfaction
Customer satisfaction
Positive impact on society

Empowerment

A major benefit of knowledge management is empowerment. The fact that everyone has to contribute and share ownership of community knowledge reduces the practice of concealing knowledge in the interest of building a personal power base through non-shared knowledge. It is obviously in the company's interest to promote sharing of knowledge, intelligence and ideas, to blow away these vested interests. Some staff will feel that they are vulnerable if everyone else understands the process they operate and their contacts, particularly in the consultancy partnership style of environment.

One manifestation of this negativity towards KM is the "not invented here" syndrome, whereby people don't always want to follow up an idea because it wasn't theirs. This is anathema to the concept of KM, which is focused on sharing and building. One way to reduce this is to do what Tube Investments did when they created an annual "not invented here" award for the best borrowed idea.

HOW SHOULD A MARKETER APPROACH KNOWLEDGE CREATION?

The best way to get KM off the ground in any organisation is to choose an area of common interest to a broad audience, and to then document and circulate information. The brands are the best starting point. It is important to build an internal web of knowledge around the key brands and encourage other members of the marketing, sales, finance, development and administration teams to add to it. Enhance this with customer and competitor views if known, and research for external studies on the brand. It's also worth asking what the brand means to individuals in the company, to see if there is a common view of brand values. In this way it is possible to start a community linked by a common interest. The knowledge marketer's role is to keep the "wheels on the bus" and sustain the enthusiasm until a network is created. The role is very much what US academics would term a "knowledge activist" role. They should:

1. Act as a catalyst to knowledge creation, and ask the right questions or triggers, i.e. who, when, what, why, how and where?

2. Look for connections between knowledge provided.
3. Use it to "guide" the future activities and strategy.

Checking out the knowledge base should become part of the process of any new product, or activity. For example, Johnson & Johnson's pharmaceutical research company review knowledge gained as part of the NPD process. Similarly, both Ford and IBM work in groups to share knowledge and experience to solve new R&D dilemmas. In the area of product knowledge, companies such as Sony and 3M introduce hundreds of new products per annum through creative knowledge sharing. This can produce significant time and cost savings when you consider that for a manufacturer, R&D budget can be 10% of the company's turnover.

The process is shown in Figure 5.1:

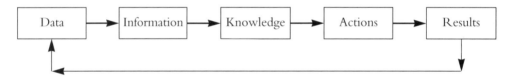

Figure 5.1   Creative knowledge sharing.

Technology

The enabler is obviously the technology. However, according to IBM, unfortunately there are now over 2000 different software packages for KM. These can vary from basic information management systems or contact management organisers to extensive intranet applications with key search and e-CRM technology, complete with network community areas. The process of selection can be narrowed down by visiting experts on the technology online, for instance www.muscat.com or www.knowledgeshop.com where it is possible to browse for document management systems, gurus, consultants and helpful conferences. There are also a number of publications, for instance, *Knowledge Management* magazine, www.knowledgemanagement.co.uk.

You will want to consider:

- The design and architecture of the online work space – what it looks like, and how you navigate around it, how you index and search for documents, and wildcard searches.
- Have intelligent searching facilities, through the incorporation of an intelligent agent which will be able to match concepts and contextual relationships, instead of just matching words. For instance, it can decipher whether you are looking for apples or Apple computers.
- Whether to have open chat areas – there are pro's and con's. Whilst it is very useful to have chat areas, and also very customer focused. However, there are issues that the company are responsible for content and, therefore, the site will need to be regularly monitored for defamatory comments.
- How intervention and moderation of data will take place.
- Tools for visual communication.
- How to organise content so that some areas are available for viewing by suppliers or customers (extranet) and others for employees only (intranet).
- eCRM enablement: this will mean that whenever an individual logged on to the site/space they would be able to save documents to their own Web area, and the Web manager would be able to send relevant information to them, or send key messages as a type of e-mail.

Some Guidelines

Simple ways of improving information storage:

1. Always produce contents and an index for information, to make things easy to retrieve.
2. Stick to a common format.
3. Put a "next revised" date so people know when it is modified or added to.
4. Seek advice from professionals, for instance, from the Chartered Institute of Marketing's librarians.

The information could for instance be codified into:

1. working knowledge
2. mistakes
3. learning and change in circumstance
4. contracts.

Valuable information for marketers needs to be updated and used regularly, to help with, for instance:

1. Success/failure of campaigns or products/services/sponsorships, partnerships.
2. Key account contacts, opinions, focuses.
3. Knowledge of the key customers, planning cycles, financial success of products.
4. Relative success of inputs from various agencies, consultants, key contact.
5. Who in the team worked on which projects and who works best together.

6. What measurements were employed?
7. What went wrong?
8. Could the project be repeated? What would have to be done better? For example, more or less resource, different strategy or tactics, different focus, different execution?
9. Rank the overall success of the project out of 10.

In addition:

1. Collaboration is essential and is a people issue.
2. Benchmark where the organisation is now, and then start to build on this.
3. Knowledge is a resource; you need to manage content to maximise yield.
4. Marketing needs to have a strategy for using and dealing with the information.

The knowledge management system should include the following:

1. Manage the generation of knowledge through learning.
2. Capture knowledge and experience.
3. Share, collaborate and communicate knowledge.
4. Organise information for easy access.
5. Use and build on what is known.
6. Develop tools and processes i.e. try to standardise what your company does in the future, but keep the door open to change if new knowledge becomes apparent.

THE BENCHMARKING PROCESS

1. Identify several similar companies to yourself in non-competing sectors. They should have similar supply chains and customers.
2. Seek agreement with them to swap data confidentially on sales, customer satisfaction, margin, key account profitability, Web effectiveness, campaign effectiveness, process management e.g. time, people, other resources, department costs, training and advertising spent, etc.
3. Swap data on a pre-agreed basis e.g. quarterly, with an annual review.
4. Create templates and meet occasionally.
5. Benchmark against competitors, based on tracking their sales, annual reports, trade intelligence research and advertising campaign monitoring. Talk to the supply chain including your own customers.
6. But, do not form an information-swapping arrangement with direct competitors; these could be viewed as a cartel which is illegal.

It is also important to benchmark data, and establish where a company is now. This can be gleaned from a number of sources:

1. Previous presentations, reports and journals.
2. Collective knowledge of agencies and current management, including sales force.
3. Knowledge of partners and associates, trade/distributors.
4. Databanks, audits, financial information.
5. Libraries, catalogues, public domain case studies.
6. Manuals, memos, strategy and policy documents.
7. Training.

Knowledge is obviously time-critical and has to be relevant. The skill is in deciphering experience and making it relevant in the future. Knowledge stored on an extranet knowledge area, may have been gleaned over time (several years) and space (e.g. from a UK sales force, Indian call centre, US marketing team, distribution channel in Asia).

The key requirements in using the technology are:

1. Summary pages of no more than 200 words, linked to relevant knowledge content and similar subjects, so users can drill down to access deeper information and add their own comments.
2. Segmentation into projects, strategy documents and bulletins.
3. Searchable database by type of product/service, type of activity, customer records and a general word-search.
4. Accessibility, scroll and navigability, usability.

To access the value of a company's KM system in solving problems, ask yourself the following questions:

1. What is the lowest acceptable profit before product/service is discontinued? What sign-offs or loan extensions could be made?
2. What structures and processes are preventing the implementation of good ideas?
3. Have we benchmarked and saved costs wherever possible?
4. Has KM resulted in improved performance and time?
5. Have opportunities to form partnerships been taken up?
6. Are there any supply chain or process issues?

THE ROLE

1. Must have a basic knowledge of technologies involved, and be able to work on the creation or ongoing development of the Web space/intranet.

2. The individual senior brand marketer should to have the skills to:

    a) manage, and provide and cajole fellow managers to provide information updates. The individual must command respect.

    b) run campaigns.

    c) strategically analyse content.

3. Project-manage content creation.

4. Input to strategy in all campaigns.

5. Liaise with "knowledge owners" in other departments.

6. Monitor progress and keep stakeholders involved.

Stakeholders	Customers	Suppliers
CEO	Marketers	IT vendors
Marketing directors		IT department
Sales team		
Other departments		
Agencies		
IT department		

CORE COMPETENCIES

1. Copywriting skills.

2. Strategic thinker.

3. Team player.

4. Command respect.

5. Attention to detail.

6. Project organising skills.

7. Communication skills.

SUMMARY

1. This chapter has introduced the concept of KM and its importance to the marketing team.

2. KM is at the heart of innovation and NPD. It can help stimulate creativity, and save time, effort and money by not repeating the same mistakes. It provides a strong research basis for decision-making and helps in measuring and benchmarking success or failure.

3. Surveys indicate that it is a hot topic on the management radar screen.

4. The technology is only the framework. The important thing is to receive contributions from everyone, and use the data received as a decision aid. Linking contribution to reward schemes is a great incentive.

5. This is not just a fad, it is important.

6. We need it as a tool for reducing process cost and for competitive advantage.

7. There are many examples of successful implementation across many sectors.

8. Managers need to lose the "not invented here" attitude, and be positive about failure, learning from their mistakes.

9. Marketers have a key role in the process. It will also help to give credibility to the department, in terms of being more measurable.

10. Plan how you frame the content: include "revised dates" functionality and data search.

USEFUL SOURCES

Allee, V. (1997) *The Knowledge Evolution: Expanding Organisational Intelligence*, Butterworth-Heinemann.

Davenport, T. and Prusak, L. (1997) *Information Ecology: Mastering the Information and Knowledge Environment*, Oxford University Press.

Davenport, T. and Prusak, L. (1997) *Working Knowledge: How Organisations Manage What They Know*, Harvard Business School Press.

Nonaka, I. and Takeuchi, H. (1995) *The Knowledge-Creating Company*, Oxford University Press.

Peters, T. (1992) *Liberation Management*, Balletine Books.

Peters, T. (1988) *Thriving on Chaos*, Macmillan.

Prusak. L. (ed.) (1997) *Knowledge in Organisations: Resources for the Knowledge-Based Economy*, Butterworth-Heinemann.

Stewart, T. (1997) *Intellectual Capital – The New Wealth of Organisations*, Nicholas Brealey Publishing.

Wilmott, H. (1998) *Knowledge Management: A Real Business Guide*, Caspian Publishing.

Books – Intranet

Although there are a great many books on intranet design, the two recent titles listed here are unusual because they deal with the management of intranets.

Bernard, R. (1998) *The Corporate Intranet*, second edition, John Wiley & Sons.

Gonzalez, J. (1998) *The 21st Century Intranet*, Prentice Hall.

TRAINING

Chartered Institute of Marketing – www.cim.co.uk

HELPFUL WEBSITES

www.assistum.com – UK software company.

www.brint.com/orglrng.html – US-based KM portal.

www.delphigroup.com – US research group looking at KM sites.

www.efqm.org/bluefrom.htlm – European Foundation for Quality Management

www.knowledgebusiness.com/home/indix.asp – A US Web community for knowledge-based organisations.

www.knowledgeinsight.com – Insight Technologies is a computer software company with KM tools for the Internet.

www.knowledgeshop.com – Purchase useful books and research materials online.

www.mcb.co.uk/jkm.html – Own the Emerald database of management-focused content.

www.mgmt.utoronto.ca – University of Toronto site containing KM research section.

www.tfpl.co.uk/areas of expertise/knowledge-management.html – Leading consultants in London and New York.

www.tlainc.com/jkmp.html – The Leadership Alliance (TLA) is a US publisher of the *Journal of KM Practice*.

www.vistacompass.com/ikm public/index.html – The Institute of Knowledge Management.

THE PARTNERSHIP MARKETER

THE PARTNERSHIP MARKETER

T his chapter considers the importance of building and managing partnerships with other brands. As the customer becomes more of a focus across the whole organisation, and the customer becomes more powerful, it is worthwhile building and developing partnerships with other brands that are linked to the preferences of the target consumer. So, for instance, it is possible to link with brands based on lifestyle – an example would be that Coca-Cola may be a good partner for Nike. Wherever products could be clustered or bundled to appeal to the same target consumer, there may be merit in forming a partnership to reduce costs and increase consumer benefit.

Whilst a partnership is not the only option, it is often the only realistic one. The list below shows options for working with other companies.

Alliances — Often a standoff to agree trade patterns and non-competition.

Partnership	–	Benefit of synergy in brand offering to the benefit of company and consumer. Can be short term.
Merger/Acquisition	–	More long term, often more expensive, not always to consumers' benefit.
Sponsorship	–	Much looser arrangement.
Promotions	–	Very short-term, time-sensitive product relationship.

Building on lifestyle attributes is particularly popular, especially on Websites, and this can be done up or down the supply chain or across different products. Amazon are a good example, where any site can become a partner and receive a percentage of Amazon's revenue for the number of users clicking through to Amazon's site from theirs.

This in turn has led to "co-opertition" where companies both collaborate and compete simultaneously, for instance, a car manufacturer and a bank, who lend finance for the customer to buy the vehicle.

These partnerships can be beneficial if managed properly. The issue is that activity should be co-ordinated so that the whole marketing team, and the rest of the organisation, are aware of the "when, who, why and what" of the partnership agreement. In this chapter, we will consider issues of partnership, marketing alliances and co-operation, and draw together a summary of the role and job description attributes for this matrix function.

PARTNERSHIPS

Increasingly, companies are looking for online and offline partnerships, some-times relationships formed as a product of mergers or takeovers such as

Centrica and AA, or CNN and AOL. However, mutually beneficial relationships can develop without such extremes. A good example would be the relationship between Procter & Gamble and Coca-Cola, discussed in the next section.

Procter & Gamble and Coca-Cola

Procter & Gamble recently announced an alliance with Coca-Cola — which offered the brand owners a model for collaboration instead of competition.

The two giants claimed that this was a "marriage made in heaven". The deal creates a new worldwide company to market and distribute P&G's Sunny Delight, Pringles snacks and Puncia soft drink alongside Coke's Minute Maid, HI-C, Fruitopia and Five-Alive juice drinks and a number of other smaller Coke drinks brands.

Such a partnership is often unpopular with the competition. In this example one UK observer noted "It sounds very cartel-like — bringing together two massive companies which are both committed to market domination and which control a huge proportion of the global industry."

What it does is suggest in relation to the direction global brand marketing will take is that more and more companies will consider partnerships as a core strategic element of planning in the twenty-first century. It combines Coke's unrivalled distribution channels through small shops with P&G's expertise in new product development.

Another observer stated, "What I don't get is why Coke wants to tie up with P&G which has been a tough rival with Sunny Delight for some time." The answer is clearly that the benefits of operational synergies, customer target, and cost advantage by channel sharing, exceed the inconvenience of conflict on one product line.

Tim Ambler of the London Business School believes, however, that, "If I were the Chief Executive, I could not cope working for both P&G and Coke at the same time. Given that they both have such strong marketing cultures, I only see this working if the Chief Executive is given the power to create a new, separate corporate culture."

The point is that the relationship needs *managing*, which is a core function of the partnership manager.

CO-OPERTITION

Co-opertition refers to the situation where two firms are involved in and benefit from both co-operation and competition simultaneously – both types of relationships need to be emphasised at the same time.

The term "co-opertition" was coined in the early 1990s by Ray Norda, founder of Novell Corporation. The name comes from a blend of co-operation and competition. In 1996, academicians Adam Brandenburgher of the Harvard Business School and Barry Nalebuff of the Yale School of Management wrote a best-selling book on the topic. The concept has been primarily studied and deployed in the IT industry.

However, individuals within the firm can only act in accordance with one of the two logics of interaction at a time, and hence the two parts have to be divided between the individuals within the company. For instance, a product manager may be marketing the finance solutions for hire purchase within the company, whilst the partnership manager develops the relationship with other leading links.

In studies concerning buyer–seller relationships within networks, the trade-off between co-operation and competition has been emphasised as a means of creating progress among individuals involved in long-term relationships. In a sense, this century, everything is up for grabs; traditional enemies can become allies. A good example of this is Autobytel, where leading car manufacturers GM and Ford co-operate to create a new channel to market, to sell cars direct, but compete within the site to generate "stickiness" around their own products.

Competition is described as the direct rivalry that develops between firms due to the dependency that structural conditions within the industry give rise to, whereas co-opertition is the dyadic and paradoxical relationship that emerges when two firms co-operate in some activities, such as in a strategic alliance, and at the same time compete with each other in other activities.

Examples of co-operative relationships

We have mentioned the scenario of a car manufacturer and a bank, where the former sells cars, and the latter grants loans for purchasing the car. Similarly, a computer manufacturer can establish a co-operative relationship with a software producer.

A precondition for co-opertition is that individuals participate in collective actions to achieve common goals. In other words, everyone involved must (a) be on-side, seeking a common goal; and (b) understand the terms of reference, i.e. the circumstances under which they co-operate versus those under which they compete.

Co-opertition classically exists when a company that competes against another in one field, co-operates with it in different spheres. This can happen both at a political level and on a global scale. For instance, we see co-operation between the US and Russia – Russia wants to win Western support to join and participate in Western institutions (trade, credit and debt rescheduling), yet at the same time it sells arms to enemies of the US, opposes US national missile defence plans and vaguely threatens action should NATO expand further.

THE EFFECT OF THE CONNECTED ECONOMY

The Information Age has brought forth a new business form: fluid congregations of businesses – sometimes highly structured, sometimes amorphous – that come together on the Internet to create value for customers and wealth for shareholders.

When Jeff Bezos, founder and CEO of Amazon, says that people are the most valuable corporate asset, he's not just talking about his employees, but about the authors, customers, suppliers and everyone else who adds value to the Amazon business web. Cisco is a similar story. You don't have to own all the elements of the Web business, but you must have the best assets and the best reach and access through partners.

CHOOSING PARTNERS

1. In choosing partners, the first requirement is to identify your core competence and learn how to co-operate with potential partners to further strengthen your reach and feasible Internet ideas.
2. Consider customer needs, and segmentation of your customer. What are the defining characteristics of your customers? What else do they buy, and therefore who would make a best-fit partner?

3. Consider your product range. Could they satisfy the needs of customers you cannot easily reach? Can another brand owner, through a partnership reach that consumer better than you can? This could be through their power in the channel to market, through brand association or, for instance, by the strength of their database.

4. Create a shortlist of potential partners and weight them based on potential added value to your brand, good fit with your company, and synergistic value. What else could you do together to build on the proposition?

5. Discuss opportunities with the relevant companies, preferably direct, cutting out intermediaries.

Example – the smartcard industry – discussed by a key marketing director – is not an industry in which you can say:

OK, I can do it all. I don't need anybody else. I'll provide you with the infrastructure, the cards, the software and so forth.

Instead competitors should work together – not as competitors, but people wanting to promote an industry. If you have three main companies in a whole market, there's enough for everyone to get their own piece of the pie. When it comes to loyalty we share some of the same partners. One of our partners is also one of their partners.

Refusing to do business with another company because it competes with you in other business lines makes no sense. If an insurer has a product banks can sell, regardless of whether the insurer competes with the banks on another product, the bank should sell it – because it will help them make money.

Quite frankly, a lot of us are fighting over the same traffic sources, a lot of us are fighting over the same dealers and shipping leads to each other back and forth. There's an increasing need to bring players together.

THE IMPORTANCE OF CO-OPERATION

To emphasise the importance of co-operation we will look at two surveys. First, a recent international PricewaterhouseCoopers survey shows an increasing shift towards working together in partnership along the production and sale process, from suppliers at one end to consumers at the other. Most survey respondents believe that barriers to co-opertition or partnering are being overcome, and predict a shift towards partnerships in the next five years. Responses on whom organisations expect to partner with are far more intriguing. Eighty per cent felt that, within five years time, they would be partnering within non-competing organisations.

Fifty per cent of total respondents thought that they would be partnering, on certain aspects, with their competitors, while 90% thought that they would be in some form of business partnership arrangement with customers and suppliers.

In other words, half of the businesspeople surveyed believe that co-operation is the way of the future, while an overwhelming majority expect to be working within more tightly and better integrated supply chains than they do at present.

Imagine two hypothetical breweries in a fierce battle for national market share teaming up to improve efficiency, lower costs and prices and expand reach through co-ordinated distribution. In other words, forget your cut of the cake, and concentrate on making the overall cake larger.

Second, a recent Ernst and Young survey of computing and electronics business leaders suggests that CEOs are focusing more than ever on savvy partnership-building. More than 66% expect to increase marketing, technology licensing, joint product development and distribution alliances over the next five years. More than two thirds say that alliances are crucial to their future plans.

Most want to access new markets, while others see enhanced distribution as the key to developing partnerships.

Almost three-quarters recognise that partnerships fail primarily because of overly optimistic expectations, poor communications and lack of shared bene-fits. "Press release partnerships" are more a triumph of hope than mutual com-mitment. Also, alliances should not be used as a substitute for strategy.

Most agree that contracts don't cover close relationships, which is what a partnership must be about if it hopes to survive. Trust, commitment and trans-parency are more important if one sees the partnership as part of a broad, long-term aim.

There must also be shared risk and shared reward. Risk means that you develop as part of the partnership's interdependency so that both parties have to deliver. It's not a one-way situation.

Although partnerships are becoming increasingly popular, as with any arrangement there is a downside. In the intellectual property business unwind-ing a partnership can be very difficult because it's hard to break up or dismantle ideas and say: "This is ours, not yours". It must be very clear from the start who owns what. This contract is a key responsibility of the partnership manager.

RELATIONSHIPS BETWEEN COMPETITORS

Intense competition is argued to be a central driving element in pressuring and stimulating firms to innovate and upgrade their competitive advantage. Proxi-mate competitors are able, within a short space of time, to observe each other's moves and counter-moves, enabling them to rapidly imitate each other's products. Psychological factors, such as prestige and pride, also stimulate com-panies to compete actively and to be innovative in their actions. In this way, rivalry sharpens the struggle and therefore increases the dynamics within an industry.

FORMING SUCCESSFUL CO-MARKETING PARTNERSHIPS

The type of arrangement that is of most interest to the marketer is when the opportunity is created to jointly market a brand, product or service.

Co-marketing partnerships between firms afford fresh opportunity for strategic advantage. Gains in effectiveness can be obtained by reducing power and managerial imbalances. Careful project selection and better matching of potential also help to enhance effectiveness.

For instance, in 1991 Apple and IBM announced a strategic alliance to share technologies. By this move, IBM expanded its influence into certain classes of personal computers, which it would be unlikely to achieve through internal development, and Apple Computers obtained improved connectivity to mainstream corporate computing.

Co-marketing agreements are a form of working partnership: "mutual recognition and understanding that the success of each firm depends in part on the other firm" (Anderson and Narus 1990). They are contractual relationships undertaken by firms whose respective products are complementary in the marketplace. They are intended to amplify and/or build awareness of benefits derived from these complementarities.

Unlike buyer/seller or manufacturer/distributor relationships, co-marketing relationships are lateral relationships between firms at the same level in the value added chain, and represent a form of "symbiotic marketing" (Adler 1966, Vardarajan and Rajaratnam 1986).

Microsoft used its alliance with IBM for the MS-DOS operating system in the early 1980s to catapult itself into the position of the dominant PC software firm. Alliances such as this are common in high-technology industries in which even the largest firms cannot hope to maintain cutting-edge positions across all technologies of interest to their end users.

So, co-marketing partnerships present opportunities, but also significant management challenges. The potential for serious conflict is always present, as partners often compete with each other in other product lines and, on occasion, in those directly covered by the co-marketing agreement.

NURTURING PARTNERS

The performance of a partnership ought to be dependent on the partners' ability to mitigate any power imbalance between them. The presence of a power imbalance creates the potential for conflict.

Another dimension of project management is that members of an alliance are likely to be sensitive to the contributions made by their partners – i.e. concern for equity in pulling one's weight.

My hypotheses are that:

1. Power imbalance in a co-marketing alliance is related negatively to the effectiveness of the relationship.
2. Therefore, managerial imbalance in a co-marketing alliance is related negatively to the effectiveness of the relationship.
3. However, the higher the project payoff from a co-marketing alliance, the greater the effectiveness of the relationship.

4. The greater the organisational compatibility between the firms in a co-marketing alliance, the greater the effectiveness of the relationship.
5. The longer and more stable the prior history of business relations between partners in a co-marketing alliance, the greater the effectiveness of the relationship.
6. The greater the age of a co-marketing alliance, the greater the effectiveness of the relationship.

It is crucial for success that four characteristics of co-marketing agreements are agreed up-front:

1. formality: who is subservient to whom? Is it a level playing field? What is the relative role of the management teams?
2. Exit barriers: Under what circumstances can partners pull out, and in what time period?
3. Exclusivity: can others join the relationship group?
4. Financial incentives and relative rewards for partners.

There has to be collaborative advantage. In fact, being a good partner has become a key corporate asset.

FUNDAMENTAL ASPECTS OF BUSINESS AGREEMENTS

Let's now look in more detail at the fundamental aspects of business agreements:

1. The partnership must yield benefits for the partners, but it is more than just a deal. They are living systems that evolve progressively. Beyond the

immediate reasons they have for entering into a relationship, the connection offers the parties an option on the future, opening new doors and unforeseen opportunities.

2. Partnerships have to involve collaboration (creating new value together), rather than mere exchange (getting something back for what you put in). Partners value the skills each brings to the alliance.

3. They cannot be "controlled" by formal systems, but require a dense web of interpersonal connections and internal infrastructures which enhance learning.

4. Successful partners build and improve a collaborative advantage by first acknowledging and then effectively managing the human aspects of their alliances.

5. Partnerships could include:

    (a) pooling resources to gain a benefit too expensive to acquire alone – access to advanced technology, for example.

    (b) joint ventures: companies pursue an opportunity that needs a capability from each of them – the technology of one and the market access of another.

    (c) value chain partnerships – supplier/customer relationships.

Successful alliances generally unfold in five overlapping phases:

1. Courtship: two companies meet, are attracted and discover compatibility.
2. Engagement: they draw up plans and close the deal.
3. Honeymoon: the companies discover they have different ideas about how business should operate.
4. Marriage: bridging those differences and developing techniques for getting along.

5. Partners: old-marrieds, each company discovers it has changed internally as the result of its accommodation to the ongoing collaboration.

Companies need to look for three key criteria in a potential partner:

1. chemistry,
2. self analysis,
3. compatibility.

RULES FOR CO-OPERATION

- Don't enter into partnering arrangements merely for press releases or credibility.
- Often people use alliances and announcements as a blocking mechanism, or a barrier to entry for competitors in the market.
- A coalition is not a strategy – it's a means to achieve a strategy. Without a specific objective, you're doomed to fail.
- The benefits of any kind of combination have to be at least ten times what you think they are because the costs will be five times what you think they are.
- Keep things simple.

The characteristics of effective intercompany relationships challenge many decades of Western economic and managerial assumptions. In fact, intercompany relationships work best when they are more family-like and less rational. Obligations are more diffuse, the scope for collaboration is more open, understanding grows between specific individuals, communication is frequent and intensive and the interpersonal context is rich. The best organisational relationships, like the best marriages, are true partnerships that tend to meet certain criteria, the eight "I's".

- Individual excellence – all key personnel must believe in the partnership, and be incentivised.
- Importance – must be a core item on the CEOs agenda.
- Interdependence – there must be a reason to "need" to work together.
- Investment – must have financial backing
- Information – should diffuse and be passed freely between companies.
- Integration – must think and act as one unit.
- Institutionalisation – must be equally accepted by both managements.
- Integrity – must be a sound business need underpinned by mutual trust.

Partnership, therefore, implies mutual benefits and success, and the concept is inherently positive.

ALLIANCES

Some alliances may be very successful, but they are looser in structure than partnerships, and the implication may be that a number of alliances may pull out in the future. For instance, in the airline industry, most airlines are in some form of alliance, to fulfil loyalty points and share infrastructure and processes.

The powerful Star Alliance boasts 13 strong airlines. In competition to this British Airways (BA), American and five other airlines belong to the One World Alliance. The Alliances are relatively unstable in that members can change allegiances. Airlines around the world rushed to find new partners following United Airlines' move to buy US Airways. Other big American and European airlines may well be forced to make acquisitions or merge to expand their national or global networks and remain competitive.

Alliances are therefore different. They often involve a large number of players, and can be formed defensively as a barrier to entry. It is not always clear that members collaborate efficiently or inherently trust each other.

THE ROLE

1. Considering possible partners for future collaboration in line with corporate and brand strategy. Make recommendations to marketing director.

2. Where partnerships are agreed, take on responsibility for pan marketing project co-ordination and construct with legal support, a mutually acceptable contract.

3. Disseminate joint venture plans to management and the marketing team.

4. Liaise with partner representatives and their marketing team to develop teamwork.

5. Outline action plans to enact joint strategy and ensure consultations take place with all relevant parties.

6. Monitor progress, keeping stakeholders involved, and develop activity with relevant agencies.

7. Benchmark and measure achievements and create knowledge base for future intelligence. Feed back results to stakeholders.

Stakeholders	Customers	Suppliers
CEO – both companies	Marketers/PR team	Relevant agencies
Marketing directors (both companies)	Sales team	Promotional companies
Sales team (both companies)	Retailers/Service providers	Partner
Staff – both companies	Consumers	

CORE COMPETENCIES

1. Negotiation skills.

2. Listening skills.

3. Good team-worker/team-player.

4. Attention to detail.

5. Good disseminator.

6. Planning/project management ability.

7. Communication skills with multiple stakeholders.

SUMMARY

1. This chapter has introduced the idea of a partnership-focused marketing role as a matrix role for a marketer. We have looked at the differences between alliances and partnerships, and indicated that building partner relationships is much more involved, and requires great skill to get the best of it.

2. Co-opertition can exist where you compete with another company at one level, but can co-operate on certain products, services or aspects of business.

3. Online opportunities have acted as a catalyst to partnership building because brands can now reach new markets and new consumers, and because often the technology is more cost-effective if shared between partners.

4. To choose partners, it is necessary to look for synergy in customers, technology, product or channel.

5. Sometimes an industry can work together synergistically for the benefit of the whole industry – making the cake bigger.

6. Co-marketing partnerships, where two companies share marketing, can be very beneficial to both parties, as long as there is a shared strategic direction and managerial balance.

7. It is important that a contract exists and defines formality, exit barriers, exclusivity and financial incentives.

8. The partnership must open new doors and opportunities; it should not be simply a sales promotion.

9. The partnership development goes through five phases. It is a relationship and must be nurtured. The human aspects must be effectively managed.

10. The relationship must be built on the 8 "i's", Individual excellence, Importance, Interdependence, Investment, Information, Integration, Institutionalisation, and Integrity.

USEFUL SOURCES

Adler, L. (1966) "Symbiotic Marketing". Harvard Business Review **44**, Nov–Dec, 59–71.

Anderson, J. C. and Narus, J. A. (1990) "A model of distributor firm and manufacturer firm working partnerships". *Journal of Marketing*, **54**, 42–58.

Badaracco, J. (1991) *Knowledge Link: How Firms Compete Through Strategic Alliances*, HBS Press.

Brandenburgh, A. (1996) *Inside Intel*, HBR

Child, J. and Faulkner, D. (1998) *Strategies of Co-operation: Managing Alliances, Networks and Joint Ventures*, Oxford University Press.

Dos, Y. and Hamel, G. (1998), *Alliance Advantage: The Art of Creating Value Through Partnering,* HBS Press.

Hanan, M. (1992) *Growth Partnering: How to Build your Company Profits By Building Customer Profits*, Amacom.

Lewis, J. (1996) *Connected Corporation: How Leading Companies Win . . .,* Free Press.

Lynch, R. (1989) *Practical Guide to Joint Ventures and Corporate Alliances*, John Wiley & Sons.

Narus, J. (1998) *Business Marketing*, HBR.

Varadarajan, P. R. and Rajaratnam, D. (1986) "Symbiotic marketing revisited". *Journal of Marketing*, **50**, 7–17.

CHAPTER 7

THE METRICS MARKETER

THE METRICS MARKETER

*T*his chapter focuses on the metrics marketer, the weights and measures conscience of the marketing team. Even today, few companies operate with solid reliable metrics and data which bottom out the company's performance in terms of marketing internally and externally. Even fewer link measurement to strategy. This chapter reviews issues around what should be measured by the metrics marketer both on- and offline, and concludes with a suggested metrics plan for a fictitious company, and the role, fit and competencies to succeed in this role.

Imagine a world in which public companies could present accounts in any way, style or form to the stock markets around the globe. Or a world in which you could opt out of presenting anything at all to shareholders. It would be ridiculous, but why? The accounts give a reflection of where we are now, or have come from. They give little indication of the needs of brand development now or for the future, and only a short-term view of profitability. What is equally important is new product development (NPD), marketing investment in brands, medium-term potential, and audited market shares. None of this information is required by law, or even by shareholders, seemingly.

It is tempting for companies to hide behind the fact that they don't want their competitors to know their marketing strategy. This doesn't wash any more. In an age where information is increasingly traded and given away on the Web, marketers are increasingly aware of their competitor's activities. A more relevant question to these CEOs would be, "Do YOU know your marketing strategy?"

Myth: We know our brand shares, profitability by product, our household penetration in advertising; we even know our competitor's brand shares, we don't need to measure anything else.

This is actually the bare minimum one would expect a self-respecting marketing team to measure. There are arguments for many measures, some broad, some industry-specific, however, key measurements should include:

1. *Overall impact on society i.e. brand reputation* – Shell have had to lead the way in eco-awareness out of necessity following the rise of Greenpeace.
2. *Reputation with stakeholders* – What do customers, suppliers, the city or Wall Street and, most importantly, employees think of you?
3. *Reliability/quality/dependability* – All these are measures of consumer trust in the brand.
4. *Emotional appeal* – A brand like Virgin will always have the edge, because they succeed in representing lifestyle and are "people's champion" in their brand appeal to customers.

5. *Marketing spend and effectiveness* – Metrics can measure the health of the brands, including shares measured against various demographics, benchmarks versus competitors, media share of voice and appropriateness of the selection.

6. *Technological effectiveness* – To what extent is the company cutting-edge?

7. *Web enablement and model effectiveness* – Measuring Web results.

8. *Key partnerships and relationships* – Who do we have robust relationships with, and what are the benefits?

9. *Customer retention* – What is our lapse rate? Is it improving over time?

10. *Brand value* – Have we built equity and marketing value added year-on-year?

BACK TO BUSINESS

A research programme was carried out for the UK Marketing Council in 1999 by McKinsey, targeting CIM and Marketing Society members as respondents. The total number of companies that responded was 545.

The research results demonstrate that marketers themselves believe they need to go "back to basics" – and to refocus on consumers and how they behave.

The survey showed that external forces impacting on marketing included:

- formalised collaboration with other functions,
- clear and quantified metrics,
- building consumer/customer databases,
- recruiting high calibre people.

Limitations that marketers themselves identified included:

• increasing difficulty in identifying new opportunities,
• poor internal perception, including a lack of required capability and a lack of good marketing metrics.

Most marketers believe that metrics are very important, but they expose their greatest weakness. There is clearly a need to track performance metrics.

There is a growing clamour from CEOs to focus much more on marketing metrics; however, Tim Ambler of London Business School examined time spent by boards on various issues. He estimated that nine times more board time was given to discussing cash flow compared to thinking about trying to understand customers.

Twelve times more time was spent on expenditure than on customers. Only 15% of respondent companies ever had marketers on the board. If you take these out as a sub-group, those companies spend 8.8% of board time talking about customers, compared with just 7.6% of those who do not have marketers on the board.

MEASURING CORPORATE REPUTATION

The fact that businesses can have good or bad reputations is not a new concept, yet corporate reputation is still a relatively new concern among managers. Over the last five years, an increasing amount of research has been carried out on corporate reputation and this subject is attaining new status in business schools. Numerous books and journals have been dedicated to this and several major conferences on the subject now take place annually. Contrary to popular belief, it is not only marketing people who attend these events. In fact, marketing people are now in the minority, outnumbered by senior professors from leading business schools, from the fields of finance, strategy and organisation behaviour.

What has dawned on people is the realisation that there is a link between corporate reputation and shareholder value. No example has driven this point home as strongly as that of Marks & Spencer. For decades this brand seemed to have one of the best reputations in British business, yet now both its good name and share price are in the doldrums. British Airways provides a similar example. Reputations take a long time to build, but they can be wiped out very rapidly. Similar cases exist in the US; for example, Nike. Yet some companies take knocks to their reputation and bounce back, for example Microsoft and Shell. Perhaps these latter examples are protected due to a monopoly situation or because their fortunes are very closely linked to scarce assets, such as oil. Whatever the case, there is now more of a need to explain how this link between reputation and shareholder value operates.

INTANGIBLES

In this particular field, the finance specialists are at sea. They are hidebound by historical figures. "Intangibles" now make up most of the value of companies, and the race is on to identify, measure and manage these intangibles. This cluster of intangibles includes:

- intellectual property,
- monopolistic situations,
- brand equity,

- social capital,
- reputation.

But it is difficult to identify where one ends and another begins, hence the recent surge in the quest to measure corporate reputation. So where should companies start?

First, the meaning of reputation needs to be pinned down. How does it differ from corporate identity, corporate image or brand equity? All are related ideas. Corporate identity is how an organisation thinks of itself, while corporate image is how others see it. Traditionally marketers think of the logo and the livery as the visual expressions of corporate identity, and they think of projecting a corporate image via visual and verbal communication – advertisements, press releases, media stories and the like. They would claim both can be managed within the marketing function, but reputations are more than identity or image, and cannot be so easily managed. They exist only in the minds of other people, mostly outside the organisation.

Reputations go beyond brand equity, for it is not only in the minds of customers that they exist. As Charles Fombrun, perhaps the leading current exponent of reputation management, puts it:

A corporate reputation is a collective representation of a firm's past actions and results that describes the firm's ability to deliver valued outcomes to multiple stakeholders. It gauges a firm's relative standing both internally with employees and externally with its stakeholders, in both its competitive and institutional environments. At Henley Management College, we think of corporate reputation more succinctly, as the perception of the character of the business.

If business reputations exist only in the minds of all stakeholders and the general public, how can they be measured? Perhaps the best-known indicators of corporate reputation are the rankings that have been published by *Fortune* magazine since the early 1980s. These have spawned dozens of very similar rankings in other countries and other publications. But all these rankings suffer from two major limitations. They seek the views of only one or two groups of people – most often, corporate leaders and financial analysts. Second, the surveys used do not capture a broad enough range of topics that people generally take into account when reaching a judgement about a company's reputation.

To try to measure business reputations in a way that overcomes these limitations is a formidable task. If more stakeholder groups are to be included, the number of respondents must be greatly extended, particularly if the business is large and operates internationally. If many more items or issues are to be covered in the survey, it will become more complicated. This will add considerably to the complexity of the subsequent analysis when trying to make sense of the results.

THE REPUTATION QUOTIENT

The main alternative method to Fortune-type rankings has emerged only in the last year or two and is a significant step forward. It is the creation of Charles Fombrun of New York University and Harris Interactive, and is called the "Reputation Quotient". This is an attitude survey which asks about a number of attributes such as:

- Products and Services (perceptions of the quality, innovation, value and reliability of the company's products and services).
- Financial Performances (perceptions of the company's profitability prospects and risk).

- Workplace Environment (perceptions of how good the company is to work for, and the quality of its employees).
- Vision and Leadership (how much the company demonstrates a clear vision, strong leadership and takes opportunities for growth).
- Social Responsibility (perceptions of the company as a good citizen in its dealings with communities, employees and the environment).
- Emotional Appeal (how much the company is admired, respected and trusted).

This method has been used in several studies in the US, to measure the reputations of top companies in general and in particular industries. It is also being used in countries such as Australia and South Africa. But the biggest study of all is about to take place in Europe, in an eleven-country project involving the collaboration of top business schools, including Henley in the UK, Erasmus in the Netherlands, INSEAD in France, IESE in Spain, and Copenhagen Business School in Denmark. The method is being validated and refined to match each national culture and to try to eliminate bias. The resulting technique will be called the "Euro RQ" and its purpose is to seek the perceptions of the general public in each country.

Members of the public vary greatly in their knowledge of the companies whose reputations they are asked about. Some may be customers, others may be employees, investors, suppliers, or neighbours. Many will have no direct contact with the companies and gain their knowledge from the media or from other people. The question remains, therefore: whose perceptions are most important for a company? This may depend upon which strategic issues are most important at the time. For example, in a takeover contest, the perceptions of shareholders may be most important. Most commonly, however, customers and employees will be key, although these could be sub-categorised according to the issue.

When seeking to measure their reputations, companies will want to know how key stakeholders perceive them. They will want to know not only how good or bad their reputations are, but how stakeholders are likely to behave towards the company as a result. Orthodox surveys which measure customer or employee satisfaction are not much help in this respect. Recent developments in relationship marketing are much more useful, but they also need to be applied to stakeholder groups other than customers. The Reputation Quotient could be used in stakeholder reputation research, but now more specific approaches are available.

The Centre for Corporate Reputation and Relationships at Henley Management College, besides undertaking the Euro RQ study, is also refining methods of measuring reputation in key stakeholder relationships. The research analyses relationships in three related parts:

1. How the past and present behaviours, products, services and values of a business are perceived by a stakeholder.
2. How the stakeholder expects the business to behave in the future.
3. How the stakeholder expects to behave towards the business in the future.

Stakeholders can be categorised according to how intimate his/her relationship is with the business and also according to how critical the relationship is to cash flow. This final element also enables the link to be explored between reputation in key stakeholder relationships and shareholder value.

The measurement of corporate reputation has come a long way in the last few years. Current techniques have overtaken traditional measures, such as the number of column inches in the media. Marketers need to get up to speed with new techniques. If we are successful in clarifying the links between shareholder value and measures of reputation, it is not too fanciful to envisage a future in which company boards will insist that a CEO's salary should be dependent not only on financial performance, but also on how the company's reputation has fared during his time as CEO.

> *Example*: Jim Maxmin, CEO of Global Brands Inc, believes that US financial and professional organisations will shortly be expected to put measures of customer satisfaction online and in year-end accounts.

LACK OF ACCOUNTABILITY

Professor Robert Shaw believes that the *ultimate* test of marketing investment is whether it creates value for shareholders. But few marketing investments are evaluated from this perspective, and many would argue that it is almost impossible to link financial results to any specific marketing activity.

Increasingly, however, boards of directors and city analysts worldwide are dissatisfied with this lack of accountability for what are very often huge budgets.

Cranfield began to address this problem through the launch of the Marketing Value Added Club (see www.cranfield.ac.uk) formed with the support of several blue chip companies.

The Club sets out to create and test a new framework which shows how marketing systematically contributes to shareholder value, and how its contribution can be measured in an objective and comparable way.

There is an urgent need for such a framework. Not only does marketing need it, to answer the widespread accusations of poor performance, but corporate and financial strategists need it too, to understand how to link marketing activities to the wider corporate agenda. All too often, marketing objectives and strategies are not aligned with the organisation's overall plans to increase shareholder value.

WHAT'S WRONG WITH MARKETING?

Over the past decade there has been a growing storm of criticism of marketing, and widespread disappointment in the marketing concept. In 1993 an article entitled "Marketing's Mid-Life Crisis", quoted one typical CEO as saying: "Marketing is like a millstone round my neck". A Coopers & Lybrand survey, entitled "Marketing at the Crossroads", quoted another executive as saying: "Marketing is increasingly living a lie in my organisation".

Other articles predicted the death of the brand, and the rejection of marketing by Wall Street and the City. The work that marketing people do has variously been described as a profession, an art, a science, a sinister instrument of mass persuasion and a ludicrous waste of money. The term "marketing" is widely used in a pejorative sense in the media, and marketing types are frequently portrayed as false, immoral scoundrels. Yet, despite this, marketing people still see themselves as professionals, giving consumers the products they want, and practising a marketing science which creates the very lifeblood of business. Says John Stubbs, CEO of CIM: "Marketing has made impressive strides over the last five years".

Professionalism, effectiveness and, most of all, influence have grown. Government understands and supports marketing. This is hardly surprising, since most companies now have only two ways to go: grow profits by winning customers and markets, and increase productivity. Ironically productivity is almost invariably impacted by marketing. Stubbs states:

The days of pretending that takeover, business process re-engineering and sacking are serious long-term strategies are gone. Marketing is now centre stage. If you do not have better customer insights than your competitor, then your business strategy will soon be threadbare. If you don't have marketing skills, then strategy deployment will fail and marketplace success escape you.

However, there is clearly still a problem to be resolved. Research by the UK Marketing Council in 1997 for the Marketing Forum revealed that more than 75% of organisations were actively reviewing the future roles of their marketing people.

And some commentators see marketing as increasingly isolated from broader consumer issues. *Marketing* magazine commented on 24 July, 1997 that marketing "is in danger of becoming marginalised as companies switch emphasis from focusing on the brand to delivering total customer satisfaction". This view is borne out in a study of 100 of Europe's top companies by Ashridge Strategic Management Centre. They found that marketing was present in under 20% of company headquarters.

STRATEGIC MARKETING

Recent research by the consultancy Synesis has investigated the opinions of other managers about their marketing colleagues. Marketing work was described as tactical rather than strategic by 84% of marketing managers and 76% of general managers. This reflected a waste of talent, according to the marketing managers, 80% of whom said their strategic ideas were good to excellent.

Marketing managers themselves complained that they and their departments lacked time and authority for strategic planning, and were overloaded by a plethora of tactical jobs, including many information-gathering tasks of dubious importance. Performance monitoring by marketing managers also got marked down.

Eighty-one per cent of general managers have a poor opinion of marketing's performance monitoring, complaining that marketing's performance measurement is just adequate or worse. Marketers have a slightly better opinion of themselves, but 58% still see their performance measurement as just adequate or worse.

Market knowledge was rated as good to excellent by 77% of general managers and 78% of marketing managers, but as one respondent commented it was "divorced from the operational world".

Other comments arising from the research were:

- "Too much blue sky", "not enough feet on the ground", "need to get nearer the front-line".
- "Low profile", "little understanding of what the company does", "strategic thinking not aligned to reality", "an Alice in Wonderland mentality".
- "So-called marketers couldn't recognise real marketing if it hit them", "they are a bunch of salesmen, some failed", "the new real marketing people we once employed have all left".

Says Stubbs:

Despite marketing's success story, there remain weaknesses which are potentially lethal to company health. Too often we do not know who is good or bad at marketing. Marketing knowledge is patchy. Marketing metrics lag behind the general resurgence of marketing skills and, in too many companies, marketing has still not come to terms with the other key operations of the business. IT, HR and supply chain management all remain strangers. In the most backward companies, marketing is still seen as advertising and bunting. (Source – *Marketing Business*, September 2000, Better Marketing Management Supplement.)

WHAT SHOULD MARKETING BE DOING?

Stubbs says that marketing needs increased rigour and science, to use measurement, to show the link between marketing and profit and "take the message to the market"; to "get to know the most professional marketers and invest in them".

The crux of the matter lies in the failure to align marketing with the fundamental shareholder value objective. Marketing objective-setting is, in practice, murky or, at worst, downright wrong. Increasing sales volume, the most widely cited marketing objective, can easily be achieved by sacrificing profitability, for instance. Increasing profit, another commonly cited marketing objective, can also be attained in the short term by relinquishing investments for future growth.

Perhaps more worrying than comments about lack of alignment between marketing strategies and corporate objectives are charges of poor marketing professionalism. Very few marketing professionals, it seems, actually understand or know how to use the widely available strategic analysis tools that would help them to dovetail their plans with what is going on in the wider marketplace, and elsewhere in their organisations. There are numerous tried and tested tools that would be of immediate value in improving marketing's contribution to the main board agenda. These include the following:

1. Measure Shareholder Value Added

For example, financial rigour in appraising marketing objectives would be a useful start.

Financial managers have used tools such as Shareholder Value Added (SVA) for at least ten years now to support investment appraisal and resource allocation. SVA is not complicated, and it requires little more than a PC spreadsheet. However, these methods are mainly applied to capital projects and mergers and acquisitions. Although SVA is occasionally applied to calculate brand valuations, it is not widely used to support marketing decision-making.

2. Strategic Planning Cycle with Quantified Objectives

Marketing planning methods should be more strategic. Unfortunately, the annual budget cycle has a stranglehold over marketing objective setting. Studies of the marketing planning processes reveal that less than 20% of marketing professionals use strategic objective setting methods. Marketers term the acronym S.M.A.R.T., standing for:

S	=	Specific (Determinable)
M	=	Measurable
A	=	Achievable
R	=	Realistic
T	=	Time Specific

Few, however, stick to these objectives in the rush to cobble together short-term, sales-led promotions. Targets should be linked to company strategy and quantified.

3. Objectives

Objectives are predominantly short-term and have little connection with wide corporate plans for growing shareholder value, with no linked targets. Tangibles should be introduced.

4. Pan Company Resource Allocation

Resource allocation needs to be aligned with business growth. Yet there is a widespread disconnect between marketing's growth objectives and corporate cost-cutting objectives. Symptoms of this disconnect can be observed in the poor service provided by the majority of call centres, and the inadequate customer response from many Internet business ventures, which are very often set up as corporate cost-cutting ventures.

Again the treatment is conceptually easy. Yet, surprisingly, few marketing plans adequately assess their resource implications (especially not cross-functionally). Benchmarks against the industry and measurements of customer satisfaction would indicate if the level of strategy and training was correct.

5. Market Segmentation

This should be driven by customer needs and wants, according to best practice studies. These techniques are well understood in the academic world, but corporate practice still seems to be in the dark ages. Yet segmentation in practice is dominated by easily available demographic data, rather than data on actual customer behaviour, which is more difficult to obtain. Customer profitability can be measured and is also known to be a key driver of shareholder value, according to academic studies. Again, the state of marketing practice is poor. Remarkably few organisations use this vital tool.

6. Customer Retention Analysis

Customer retention analysis (CRA) and root cause customer defection analysis are widely written about. Market research firms can offer extensive data on retention and loyalty. Once more, the take-up is pitifully low.

SPEND ON MARKET RESEARCH

The low value that marketing places on measurement is brought home by looking at what marketing spends today on market research – about £500 million annually in the UK. Compare this with the amount engineers spend on research and development – more than 100 times what marketing spends on research. Or compare it with the amount one oil company recently spent on a new financial information system – £500 million – the same figure that all UK companies spend on marketing information.

DOES MEASUREMENT IMPEDE CREATIVITY?

Measuring and monitoring how marketing contributes to shareholder value in no way impedes the traditional creativity of marketing. Rather, it enormously strengthens it. Creativity isn't the sole prerogative of marketers, and appraising value isn't solely an accounting matter.

Despite their stereotypes, the best accountants, systems specialists, operational experts, and so on can think "outside the box" just as effectively as marketing types, whilst at the same time, marketers become more effective and more focused if they are held accountable for returns on marketing investment. Teamwork between marketing and the rest of the organisation will be a hallmark of the new Marketing Value Added approach.

DRIVING LONG-TERM CASH FLOW

Professor Peter Doyle of Warwick Business School in the UK believes that to make measurement more relevant, marketers need to do three things:

- clarify their objectives,
- clarify their understanding of the strategic value drivers,
- build a marketing scorecard that measures performance.

Marketing management has not understood that the only purpose of marketing is to create shareholder value. Marketing – at least in the private sector – adds value only to the extent that it contributes to a rising share price. As we have seen with P&G, Marks & Spencer, and BA, today if chief executives don't deliver on the share price they are quickly kicked out. The financial driver of shareholder value is long-term cash flow.

1. Increasing Present Value

Relevance demands marketing plans that clearly show how they will increase the present value of the firm's long-term cash flow through achieving faster growth, healthier long-term margins and investment that delivers returns that exceed the cost of capital.

2. Attractiveness and Competitive Advantage

Marketers need to identify the key strategic drivers of long-term growth and profitability. These centre on two factors: the attractiveness of the firm's markets and its competitive advantage.

3. Scorecard

Managers need to build a marketing scorecard that monitors progress on these two sets of value drivers. The measures of market attractiveness will include indicators such as prospective market growth, industry profitability and competition. Indicators of the firm's competitive advantage include:

- customer satisfaction
- customer acquisition
- defection rates.

The exact measures will depend upon the business and its strategic value drivers.

Marketing is the key to shareholder value. All the firms that have created the greatest returns to shareholders in recent years – Nokia, Dell, Hennes & Mauritz, etc – have been high-growth companies. By clearly identifying the marketing drivers of shareholder value and developing a relevant scorecard, marketing can achieve its rightful place in the boardroom.

ONLINE MEASUREMENT

Kasja (Leander) and Ernst (Malmsten) are artistic people, not scientific. If we learn one thing from Boo.com, it is that in this game you need to be more scientist than artist. (Kal Alabbasi, on the collapse of Boo.com – *Independent*, 19 May 2000.)

The Web has long been spoken of as "the most accountable medium ever", thanks to all the data that can be captured about any online marketing campaign.

The first measures to be used on the Web were hits and click-throughs. It is now, however, becoming more common to measure conversions, and trace the surfers who become purchasers.

Of course, such tracking relies on the use of appropriate software and the ability to interpret data accurately, but this is becoming the norm, with more and more clients having a clearer understanding of their campaign's return on investment (ROI).

Evaluating campaigns purely in such direct marketing-derived terms, however, does not present the whole picture. While such measures are a must-have if you are to fully understand the commercial impact of a campaign, to overlook the brand impact is to leave a potentially serious gap in your understanding.

Some people have said that the Web is no good at building brands. In isolation, as with any medium, it's undoubtedly limited in what it can do. But such a simplistic view overlooks the fact that any interaction with a brand has an impact on a consumer's attitude towards it.

ONLINE BRANDS

Since Netpoll first started researching user attitudes to new media in 1997, one of the most strongly consistent findings is the extent to which brands can be affected by their online activity. A Web user can interact with a brand and its offering to a far greater extent than in any other medium, reinforcing or undermining his pre-existing perception of the brand.

It's very difficult to track the brand impact of the average banner campaign. The only circumstances in which this has worked to date have been around larger-scale deals, most notably content sponsorships. Netpoll has worked with Sky, Sports.com and BT, among others, to establish the impact of online sponsorships. Some of the findings have entered the public domain and provide sample evidence that brand perception can indeed be positively, and measurably, enhanced in much the same way as for comparable TB campaigns.

This kind of campaign measurement will become the norm among larger-scale advertisers and sponsors. Those committing more money have a greater interest in quantifying the return of marketing investment in as many dimensions as possible, and it's in the interest of clients, site owners and agencies to ensure that this process is adopted as part of the maturing of the industry.

If nothing else, the measurement of campaign impact on the brand will be driven by the need to understand what effect marketing spend is having on the 97% of users not clicking through. (Source: *New Media Age*, 7 December 2000, p. 57.)

PROFITABILITY ON THE WEB

New Media (30 November 2000) suggests the Internet industry must look at how to generate value.

So how should we be looking at the Internet industry? Profitability, as always, should clearly be the key success criterion. Focusing on page views or the numbers of unique visitors is interesting, but not particularly helpful. More critical is the ability to value individual visitors. If companies cannot understand and measure the value of their unique customers, then they clearly have no real ability to focus on their most important customers and so have no control over their potential to be profitable in the future. Similarly, it is as absurd to view visitor or page view numbers in isolation from your competitors' performance as it is to analyse market research data, such as AC Nielsen data, on one company alone.

But, beyond this, there is still too great a focus on the Internet as a sales and marketing channel and not as a tool to root out inefficiencies and increase productivity. As everyone knows, but few appear to act upon, the Internet impacts the whole value chain.

Fleurop (Interflora in Germany) can demonstrate how the use of an integrated e-business solution has increased its profit per transaction by 500% while increasing sales substantially year on year. This is meaningful data.

So service businesses should be looking much more aggressively at whether the solutions really make any difference to their clients' businesses.

For too long they have been hiding under the immeasurability of meaningless jargon. Businesses must channel a greater percentage of Internet spend into measurement, based on clearly defined goals.

It is a commonly held belief that, as a minimum, companies should invest 10% of their budget in research and evaluation. Companies may also have to jettison some basic assumptions about Web-based trading, such as the idea that e-business always leads to lower costs. Although this assumption may hold true for the value chain as a whole, it will also be the case for some companies that costs may actually rise when doing business electronically. Why? Because the corollary of being able to do more is that more is expected of you. This may be in greater customer service demands, for instance. However, if your overall business benefits then, fine, but it's worth going the extra mile to make sure that Internet solutions really do create value.

Chris Robson, Chief Executive Officer at Syzygy AG, speaking in *Marketing* magazine (30 November 2000), hoped that the marketing media will lose their obsession with the power of online advertising and instead will lead the way in focusing on the real issues of profitability. It is time to look to common sense for solutions rather than miracles.

Jeffery Manning of Ogilvy Interactive suggests in *Revolution* magazine (November 2000)

> Too many campaigns go out without precise understandings of what levels of response we expect, what returns on investment we're seeking to create, or what new customer insights we are trying to unearth.
>
> In turn, this erodes the potential for continuous refinements of improvements to future activity – so wastage abounds. Millions of pounds are spent on marketing campaigns. But if you spent just 5% of that budget on setting up ways to measure the impact of those campaigns, the returns could be huge. With this information you can better target your audience.

The fact that, as an industry, digital agencies are becoming a bit slack on the measurement side, is particularly ironic given online advertising's direct marketing heritage.

> Not so very long ago many of the campaigns produced by agencies contained automatic plans for measurement and evaluation. Obviously, our direct market-

ing heritage is steeped in an ability to predict and evaluate customer response and conversion. The problem is that today, as an industry, we do this less and less.

It is too tempting to go for simple measurements of brand audiences, rather than drill down and measure the dynamics of your test customers.

MEASURING WEB MARKETING EFFECTIVENESS

An organisation's Website offers an unrivalled opportunity to measure significant aspects of marketing effectiveness, since customer behaviour can potentially be monitored in real time and responded to accordingly. Yet research suggests that companies are not making full use of this potential. In a November 1999 report titled "Measuring Web Success", Forrester Research asked 50 Global 2500 companies, "What metrics do you use to measure your Website's success?" The responses were:

- hits (82%)
- page views (80%)
- session Length (66%)
- visitor count (64%)
- ad banner click-through or referring site (38%)
- look-to-buy ratio (12%).

These figures suggest that even amongst large companies, the potential value of the Website as a marketing research tool has not been tapped. Few companies reported measurement of the site's role in influencing marketing outcomes, such as leads and sales, or how it shaped customers' brand perceptions.

To integrate a measurement programme into Web marketing activities is not straightforward. To start with, the demands of promoting a site and keeping it up-to-date may stretch the staff involved with Web marketing, who often also have responsibilities for other channels. The need to evaluate the Web in conjunction with these other channels rather than in isolation also poses technical and organisational problems. As a result, it is easy to suffer the symptoms of any poorly conceived marketing measurement programme:

- objectives poorly defined,
- data not collected,
- data not analysed,
- results not reported,
- corrective action not taken.

Research at the University of Derby in the UK has indicated that we need to compare the performance of the Internet channel to other channels and build a picture of how it is contributing to the business. Key parameters were:

1. *Channel promotion* – Promotion is successful if traffic is generated that meets objectives of volume and quality. Quality will be determined by whether visitors are in the target market and have a propensity for the service offered. Overall hits or page views are not enough, since a high proportion of visitors get no further than the home page! Differences in costs of acquiring customers via different alternative channels can also be assessed.

2. *Channel buyer behaviour* – Behaviour objectives will require customers to interact with the appropriate on-site marketing communications such as product information, promotions or customer service. Once customers

have been attracted to the site we can monitor, again using log file analysis, content accessed, when they visit, how long they stay, and whether this interaction with content leads to satisfactory marketing outcomes such as new leads or sales. If visitors are incentivised to register on-site it is possible to build up profiles of behaviour for different segments. Key performance ratios can be identified such as page impressions/visit and visitor sessions/unique visitors.

3. *Channel satisfaction* – Customer satisfaction with the online experience is vital in achieving the desired channel outcomes, although it is difficult to set specific objectives. Online methods such as questionnaires, focus groups and interviews can be used to assess customers' opinions of the Website content and customer service, and how it has affected their overall perception of brand.

4. *Channel outcomes* – Traditional marketing objectives such as number of sales, number of leads, conversion rates and targets for customer acquisition and retention should be set and then compared to other channels. Dell Computer (www.dell.com) records on-site sales but also orders generated as a result of site visits, but placed by phone. This is achieved by monitoring calls to a specific phone number unique to the site.

5. *Channel profitability* – A contribution to business profitability is usually the ultimate aim of Web marketing. To assess this, leading companies set an Internet contribution target of achieving a certain proportion of sales via the channel. When easyJet (www.easyjet.com) launched its e-commerce facility in 1998, it set an Internet contribution target of 30% by 2000. They put the resources and communications plan in place to achieve this and their target was reached in 1999. Assessing contribution is more difficult for a company that cannot sell products online, but the role of the Internet in influencing purchase should be assessed.

Most companies seem to start by considering volume of traffic (channel buyer behaviour) and outcomes (leads and sales) before moving on to review channel satisfaction and channel promotion.

Once a company identifies the SMART measures it wants to collect, the next stage will be to decide on the collection/reporting frequency. For example, on-site sales promotions for an e-tailer are often monitored daily or weekly; referring sites may be monitored monthly; while channel satisfaction may only be recorded periodically, perhaps before a major enhancement to the site.

ONLINE QUESTIONNAIRES

Online questionnaires are increasingly used by large companies, for example, the Epson UK site (www.epson.co.uk) illustrates how questionnaires can be used to gather information from all stages of the buying process. Interactive tools are available to help users select a particular printer, diagnose and solve faults, and technical brochures can be downloaded. Feedback is solicited on how well these services meet their customers' needs.

Despite the potential of Website measurement, achieving a unified view of how the Internet channel integrates with marketing communications, sales and service delivered through other channels is still some way off for most companies. Many of the Website analysis tools that are currently used are poor at integrating with other systems for CRM and sales. Suppliers such as Netgenesis (www.netgenesis.com) and Accrue (www.accrue.com) are currently developing systems that provide a better-integrated view of performance. The significant organisational challenges of finding the time to create and manage a measurement programme also need to be met.

PUTTING IT ALL TOGETHER

We will now create a typical set of metrics that a company might consider using.

Metrics for Fictitious plc

1. *Impact on society/Brand reputation* – Qualitative research survey annually, cross-section of known customers and target customer, key dynamics:

   Brand awareness – % this year versus % last year
   Propensity to buy
   Competitor brand awareness

2. *Reputation with stakeholders*
   Quantitative research – suppliers, employees.
   Qualitative research – key customers, stock market, journalists.
   Measure year-on-year trends, look at emotional brand value.

3. *Reliability/Quality/Dependability*
   Returns monthly, year-on-year by product or service.
   Complaints monthly, year-on-year by product or service.
   Quality control – internal measures.

4. *Effectiveness*
   Brand share £ % segments and overall market.
   Brand growth versus market and similar markets.

Competitor growth.

Media spend, brand profitability – last year, this year, forward plan.

Effectiveness of media spend – plan versus actual.

All measures need to be linked to targets in strategic plan.

5. *Technology*

   Market research on efficiency versus competitors.

   New technology available.

6. *Partners and relationships*

   List partners. Can growth be attributed to those relationships?

7. *Customer retention*

   Lapse rate versus last year.

8. *Shareholder Value Added (SVA) – Cashflow generation*

   We need to consider the average return a shareholder could achieve by investing elsewhere, let's say 6% fund growth. We then consider planned activity in each brand, and the payback. For the sake of simplicity, we will assume £1 has the same value as £1 in five years' time (accounts may want to build discounted cash flow into the model). The accountants will probably have a standard procedure for allocating overheads and costs, possibly on Activity-Based Costing (ABC). In other words, a share of costs can be directly attributed to a brand, in the same way as you would allocate say space and heating. Let's also, for simplicity, assume there is only one brand. The example shows that the brand expects to exceed shareholder expectations, driving the five-year plan.

Brand X – Simple Plan

	Y0	Y1	Y2	Y3	Y4	Total
Turnover	£10m	12m	14m	16m	20m	
Less allocated costs						
Before marketing activity	£8m	9m	10m	11m	12m	
Contribution	£2m	3m	4m	5m	8m	
Advertising – media	£2m	1.5m	1m	1m	0.5m	
– creative	£0.5m	0.5m	0.3m	0.3m	0.2m	
a) Profit	(£0.5m)	1m	2.7m	3.7m	7.3m	14.2m
Equity	10.5m					
b) Expected return (6%)	0.63m	0.67m	0.71m	0.75m	0.80m	3.56m
SVA (a−b)	−1.13m	0.33m	1.99m	2.95m	6.5m	10.64m

9. *Investment*

   Investment to sales ratio (I/S ratio).

   Investment in NPD to sales ratio.

   Investment in market research to sales ratio.

10. *Pricing*

   Average price per brand compared to largest competitor and market average.

   Price tracks over five years compared to inflation.

11. *Database*

   Number of active customers on database.

   Analyse clusters by socio-demographic segments.

   Compare year-on-year.

12. ***Other Intangibles***

Value of intellectual property year-on-year.

Estimated valuation of brand portfolio.

13. ***Online Management of Web brand activity***

Quantitative	–	Hits/Stickiness
	–	Page views
	–	Session length
	–	Visitor count
	–	Ad banner click-throughs
	–	Look-to-buy ratio
	–	Promotional take-up
	–	Sales
	–	Leads
	–	Online questionnaires
Qualitative	–	Channel satisfaction
(focus group)	–	Navigability
	–	Service or product delivery waiting time
	–	Call centre speed/attitude
Financial	–	Paybook (SVA)
	–	Sales turnover
	–	Margin
	–	Profitability

THE ROLE

1. Prepare and collate regular monthly/quarterly/annual figures for Internal audiences, and externally for website and annual reports.

2. Commission research projects to build qualitative metrics.

3. Ensure consistency of marketing reporting pan company.

4. Review and analyse metrics and management of revenue in marketing, in collaboration with the financial department.

5. Benchmark competition.

6. Impact into strategic planning and monitor actual achievement versus SMART plans.

7. Manipulate databases to produce clustered analysis of segments.

STRATEGIC FIT – TYPICAL STAKEHOLDERS AND CUSTOMERS OF JOB HOLDER

Stakeholders	Customers	Suppliers
CEO	Marketing director	IT department
Analysts	Other marketers	Research companies
Shareholders	PR executive	
Employees	Finance department	

CORE COMPETENCIES

1. Statistical analysis and mathematics.

2. Marketing campaign planning.

3. Market research skills and intelligence gathering.

4. Financial skills/training.

5. Soft skills – managing stakeholder, customers and suppliers.

6. Communication at all levels.

SUMMARY

1. Be aware of need to look at overall brand and corporate reputation and measure it.

2. Select criteria for measurement and key metrics to be used.

3. Measure intangibles – past, present, future forecast.

4. Decide reporting strategy – monthly, quarterly, annual data.

5. Differentiate between internal and external reporting.

6. Ensure strategy has SMART objectives which are quantified and monitor them.

7. Set up benchmarking, and commission consistent programme of research.

8. Monitor market, competition, and company achievements.

9. Agree sensible Web monitoring analysis.

10. Be consistent with financial accounting policy e.g. Activity Based Costing.

USEFUL SOURCES

Ambler, T. (2000) *Marketing and the Bottom Line*, Pearson Education.

Davidson, H. (1997) *Even More Offensive Marketing*, Penguin

Doyle, P. (2000) *Value Based Marketing*, Wiley & Sons.

GB Information Management (1998) *Momentum Marketing*, Incisive Research.

Fombrun, C. (1996) *Reputation – Realising Value from the Corporate Image*, HBS Press.

Fombrun, C. (March 2000) The Reputation Quotient, *Journal of Brand Management*.

HELPFUL WEBSITES

Financial Times/Pricewaterhousecoopers – the world's most respected companies 1999/2000 – www.ft.com/specials/sp41c6.htm and http://specials.ft.com/wmr2000/FT3GX6PUNGC.html

Fortune top 500 companies – America's largest organisations – www.fortune.com/indexw.jhtml?channel=list.jhtml&list fast=list 3solumn)fortune 500 list.jhtml&list=15& requestid=214540

Harris – Fombrun Reputation Quotient – www.harrisinteractive.com/pop up/rq/

Joint IAB & Millard Brown Interactive report – online advertising effectiveness study – www.mbinteractive.com/site/iab/iabstudy full.pdf

Marketing Metrics – draft paper: a review of performance measures in use in the UK and Spain – www.msi.org/msi/00-500.pdf

Shaw: Measuring and valuing customer relationships – www.shaw-wethey.com/html/measuring and valuing customer.htm

SKILLS LEVEL ANALYSIS PROCESS

Marconi and the Chartered Institute of Marketing (CIM) have developed a new system to help marketers grow, called the Skills Level Analysis Process (SLAP).

This process defines current marketing roles by title, and details the skills and knowledge profiles that are required to meet the demands of the role.

The objectives of the process are to

- facilitate staff development
- define competencies/skill levels required
- assess current skill levels in the company
- produce personal development plans

The resultant table breaks these competencies down into 18 levels, graded one to five on level of expertise.

For more details contact – marketing@cim.co.uk

INDEX